ƒ1.50

THE ROARING LIONS

Other books by J. B. G. Thomas available

RUGBY: MEN, MATCHES AND MOMENTS

SPRINGBOK INVASION

FIFTY-TWO FAMOUS TRIES

The Roaring Lions

J. B. G. THOMAS

PELHAM BOOKS

First published in Great Britain by Pelham Books Ltd
52 Bedford Square, London, W.C.1

© 1971 by J. B. G. Thomas

All Rights Reserved. No part of this publication may be reproduced, stored in a retrieval system, or transmitted, in any form or by any means, electronic, mechanical, photocopying, recording or otherwise, without the prior permission of the Copyright owner

7207 0545 2

Set and printed in Great Britain by Tonbridge Printers Ltd,
Peach Hall Works, Tonbridge, Kent
in Times ten on eleven point on paper supplied
by P. F. Bingham Ltd, and bound by
James Burn at Esher, Surrey

To the memory of
those first gallant Lions of 1904 in New Zealand,
who blazed the trail that was followed
so successfully by the fine sportsmen
of 1971

PREFACE

Many helped me in the production of this book but particularly the British Lions and their most efficient management. All New Zealand officials, journalists and photographers were most helpful during my journey through the pleasant land of New Zealand. The staffs of NAC, the several hotels, and the various provincial rugby offices, as well as officials at the grounds where matches were played were most friendly, as indeed were my friends of New Zealand Cable offices and the NZBC.

One cannot make a tour or write a book without friends and the British and New Zealand travelling press were always cheerful, but especially Vivian, Cliff and Tudor. Finally, to the Four Home Unions and the NZRU, I say thank you, and hope that this book reflects in some small way the spirit and the success of a magnificent tour which did nothing but good for rugby football.

J. B. G. Thomas
Cardiff 1971

CONTENTS

	Foreword by John Dawes	11
1	The Judgement	13
2	The Scarlet Runners	22
3	In the Beginning – Australia	42
4	First Taste of the North Island	55
5	Into the Deep South	87
6	The First Test	111
7	The Second Test	128
8	The Third Test	147
9	The Fourth Test	159
	Appendices – The Tour in figures	175

ILLUSTRATIONS

facing page

1	The 1971 British Lions	32
2	Gareth Edwards scores first try in New Zealand	33
3	The Lions' choir at Wanganui	33
4	The biggest welcome of the tour	64
5	Ray McLoughlin crashes over for his try against Waikato	64
6	The flying Welshman, John Bevan	65
7	Willie John McBride falls to save before a concerted Wellington rush	72
8	Gareth Edwards gets the ball despite a tackle	72
9	Vivian Jenkins and the author	73
10	Gerald Davies charging away against Otago	73
11	Sandy Carmichael after the Canterbury match	88
12	David Duckham dives over for one of his six tries *v.* West Coast/Buller	88
13	John Dawes and Colin Meads lead out their sides for the First Test	89
14	The victory hug!	89
15	Replacement Ray Hopkins passes to Barry John in First Test	89
16	Barry John shows his amazing skill	104
17	John McLauchlan scores the only try in the First Test	104
18	Taranaki's full-back Hill scores one of the best tries against the Lions	105
19	'The King' beats the record	105
20	Papers from home	120
21	John Dawes and John Taylor off duty	120

22	The Master Fisherman, Mike Roberts	120
23	Sid Going, 'man of the match' in the Second Test	121
24	Gareth Edwards under pressure in the Second Test	121
25	Ian Kirkpatrick making use of Mervyn Davies' shoulder in the Second Test	128
26	One of Gerald Davies' superb tries v. Hawkes Bay	128
27	Carwyn James	129
28	John Dawes	129
29	Gareth Edwards and a bashful stone maiden in Brisbane	129
30	Barry John in action	160
31	How to play rugby . . . the wrong way!	160
32	The first Lions' try in the Third Test	161
33	Barry John scores the second Lions' try in the Third Test	161

The author's thanks are due to the following whose copyright photographs have been reproduced in this book:

Perry Photographer, Wanganui: 1
Wanganui Herald: 3, 4
Evening Post, Wellington: 7, 13, 24, 25
Des Woods, Cromwell: 10
Inksters Ltd., Greymouth: 12
Ross Setford: 30
N.Z. Weekly News: 31

and also to all those other people whose help in obtaining pictures was so invaluable.

FOREWORD

by John Dawes

(Captain of the 1971 British Lions)

To be asked to write a Foreword to this book came as a surprise request, but one to which I readily agreed. The author has probably seen more top-class games over a longer period of time than any other rugby writer, or indeed any rugby player. Furthermore his analysis of the game, at all levels, has given him a great insight into the development of the 'modern' game, and it is with great authority, therefore, that he is able to write about this game of ours. To be able to write these few words is, then, an honour and a privilege.

This book, covering the happiest tour on which any player could wish to be, will undoubtedly bring a great deal of pleasure not only to rugby followers the world over, but to actual members of the 1971 Lions. Why the tour was so successful, both on and off the field, will, I am sure, be dealt with in the following pages, but credit for this success must go to many people both directly and indirectly involved.

I suppose the tour began back in 1970 with the appointment of Dr Doug Smith and Carwyn James as manager and coach respectively. Its ultimate success was, in no small way, due to the organisation, planning, dedication and knowledge with which these two gentlemen built the 1971 Lions. Never, in my experience as a rugby player, has success been so richly deserved than by these two very popular managers. Some months later, after a fantastic amount of travelling and research by Doug and Carwyn, the players chosen to represent Great Britain were announced. For the first time a Welshman was invited to captain the party. That this should happen is a direct tribute to the 1971 Welsh XV, the Welsh Squad, the Welsh coach Clive Rowlands, and not least to all those people who were responsible for the birth, and development, of coaching at national level. My own feelings were simply ones of sheer joy, and this was undoubtedly the highlight of my career. Needless to say, I was determined, along with every other member of the party, to win the series and to do it in a way which reflected the good aspects of British rugby. Fortunately the '71 Lions possessed the players with all the necessary attributes – the most important of all being skill – to see it all happen. How it all happened is covered in the following chapters.

For any person travelling on a major overseas tour, whether as a player or a reporter, or even a supporter, it is a memorable experience and one which will give everlasting pleasure. Surely a tour is 'made' by the men who make it. 'Willie John' McBride had an expression which summed up the whole attitude and welfare of the party: 'Men, it's great to travel with you.' Never has an expression been more apt! Not only was it applicable to members of the official party, but encompassed the British Press, the N.Z. Press and all those who journeyed the length and breadth of New Zealand together. I would further add that relations between Press and players could not be bettered.

As a player I shall treasure several memories – the innate skills of Barry John, Mike Gibson and Gerald Davies; the competitiveness of Gareth Edwards and John Williams; the dedication of 'Willie John'; the fantastic technical knowledge of Ray McLoughlin, who did so much to set the tour off on the right road; the enthusiasm of Gordon Brown; the frightening power of John Bevan; the temperament of Bob Hiller; and so on. Every member of the party contributed to its success. Above all else I will remember that the tour was successful because thirty-three talented players were superbly coached, guided and managed by two very talented men in their own right. Such was the respect and popularity they won from the players that long before the end of the tour the players were playing for them and not only for Great Britain.

In conclusion I say this 1971 Lions tour to New Zealand was a happy one and one for which I feel honoured and extremely proud to have been fortunate enough to be invited. It is now over – good luck to the 1974 Lions!

John Dawes

CHAPTER ONE

The Judgement

New Zealanders, without reservation, judged the 1971 Lions as the greatest touring team to visit their country and the older spectators, who had seen the mighty 1937 Springboks in action, said they were no better than these latest Lions who blazed a trail through the North and South Islands and restored to the full the true image of British rugby. For their outstanding efforts they are deserving of praise on every side – and in a world of changing ideals and standards and new attitudes towards sport, they proved conclusively that the British attitude to rugby football is a healthy one, and that it is still one of the finest amateur team games yet devised by man.

To have travelled with this side was a privilege and a delight, for their very presence, attitude and skill combined to make the visit memorable, and the lot of a travelling recorder particularly pleasant and enjoyable in one way, but extremely hard in another, since one could never supply enough copy and comment to meet the needs of hungry followers back home! Yet the delights and hazards of following a highly successful team go hand in hand and this was a trouble free tour, in an era when pressure on management and players is considerable in any sport.

It ranks with 1955 as the happiest and most successful tour of this century, as its playing record was superior to that wonderful side in South Africa, and considering that New Zealand presents a slightly more strenuous programme, it must be classed as the GREATEST of the century. Down through the years and with the passing of each Lions tour, I wondered when another side would just nose in front of Jack Siggins and his merry, much-talented party of 1955. It happened in 1971 and I am sure that Siggins, man of good taste and judgement that he is, would be the first to congratulate his successor as top manager, Douglas Smith, had he been a watcher in New Zealand!

There were three of us, professional observers with the 1971 party, who had been in South Africa during that winter of sweet content in 1955 – Cliff Morgan as the outstanding player with his infectious enthusiasm, Vivian Jenkins as the senior observer with his shrewd approach and much experience of rugby abroad, and myself as an observer 'on the road' in 1955 for the first time. Naturally, 1955 was a remarkable experience for me and those Lions gave some memorable displays in the Orange Free State match at Kroonstaad, the Transvaal match at Ellis Park, and the First Test, but I feel the 1971 side for several reasons, but mainly as a result of three special matches, against Wellington, and in the First and Third Tests, moved to the top of table of honour as the greatest.

Vivian Jenkins agrees upon this as they were a better TEAM and Cliff Morgan feels that, at their best, the 1971 side would have given his 1955 side ten points start. He believed that in 1955 there were players of equal brilliance in many positions and compared Butterfield with Gibson, and O'Reilly with Davies, Duckham and Bevan, and R. H. Williams with McBride, and so on, but that it was the tremendous dedication and organisation of approach that moved the 1971 side into the lead, as the 1955 side played their rugby 'out of the top of their heads'!

The 1924 Lions side was beset by injuries and grassless grounds; the 1930 side played much better rugby than their record suggests and almost shared the series; injuries and absence on tour of some leading players prevented the 1938 side proving itself one of the best of the century; the 1950 side lacked three additional outstanding forwards and faced rucking as a new phase in the game for the first time; the 1955 side proved tremendous and with coaching could have won the series; the 1959 side had all the talent but not quite the dedication and discipline to fulfil its potential though often brilliant; the 1962 side never really knew where it was going tactically but could have shared the series, and the 1966 side lost its way the moment it landed in New Zealand and never got out of the maze, while the 1968 side, through injuries to key players and failure to take its chances, never fulfilled its potential.

In striking contrast, the 1971 Lions knew where they were going and what they had to do from the moment they landed in Brisbane to start their tour, and the first match against Queensland, with its defeat, neither disturbed nor deterred the management and team in its objective. The plans were well laid, the team wisely selected, and the spirit generated equal to the needs of a long, exciting, arduous but highly successful tour. The object, at all times, was to play better and more successful rugby than one's opponents and dismissing the Queensland match as a 'victim' of long distance air travel with its accompanying 'dysrhythmia', it was only on one occasion, in the Second Test at Christchurch, that the opposition played the better and more consistent rugby, although even then the Lions produced some remarkable movements.

They achieved success because they achieved their potential; something that, normally, never happens in a British side for many reasons. These 1971 Lions with all their individual brilliance and flair, had team work and discipline in a far greater degree than any of the previous sides. For this there must be praise and most of it should go to Manager Smith, Coach James, Captain Dawes and senior forward McBride, with the coaching and understanding of James adding a new dimension to the British approach abroad.

At long last the Four Home Unions, under its amicable and much travelled chairman, John Tallent, and enthusiastic secretary John Hart, put their heart and minds into the task of preparing the side from the moment the management was appointed. Tallent sorted out the problem of 'job definition' for Smith, James and Dawes, and this was an important step forward, and from that moment because of the talent available in the side, success was assured. Smith had achieved an ambition after twice missing out on selection as manager, and this made his determination to succeed, all the greater.

James was one of two outstanding Welsh coaches nominated and interviewed for the post of assistant manager and coach, and his appointment produced another official, equally determined to succeed and equally well qualified, while the choice of John Dawes was not only right and proper, and could not have been avoided even by the most stern critics of Welsh rugby, and he proved a magnificent leader worthy of a place alongside Sam Walker of 1938.

The challenge was on from the start, and not only from New Zealand, smarting under the stigma of test defeat in South Africa in 1970 after a brilliant run in the provincial matches, for the appointment of James and Dawes indicated that the Welsh would be in charge, tactically, and rumour had it that the Welsh would never do well, or lead well abroad. Writers in Britain and New Zealand (Terry McLean was among them), suggested that the greatest failing of the Welsh in rugby prevented them from being good tourists, and that they were not good leaders, being inclined to 'stick to themselves' on tour. Perhaps, much of this was due to the sadness and lack of outstanding leadership in 1966 and the poor display in the tests of the 1969 Welsh touring team.

Thus whatever generated the abiding criticism that the 'Welsh must not have charge of the party on any terms' was squashed from the beginning, with the close harmony developed between Smith and James and their hard work in preparation for the tour and the desire of Smith, as chairman of the selection committee that chose the team, to have Dawes as captain. Smith wanted no one else and told his fellow selectors, although there was strong backing from Ireland for Gibson. Fortunately, Dawes was, in the end, the unanimous choice and Gibson, relieved of this responsibility as well as being unshackled mentally and physically, produced the best rugby of his career and was a truly magnificent player in the star-studded back division. At long last the great potential of Gibson was realised and this would not have happened had he been captain.

Dawes succeeded handsomely because he was an expert in captaincy. For previous tours players had been appointed as captains without any long study and practical experience of the exacting task, but six years as a successful leader of a brilliant London Welsh club side and a year leading Wales to the Grand Slam in Europe, made Dawes the ideal choice. After his selection some suggested that he would not win a test place but how little they knew of the man, who raced through the tour in superb style, taking everything in his stride and causing all to wonder and ask: 'Why was not a Welshman appointed to the job before?' At least all criticism was answered by this modest young man from Abercarn in the Valleys of Monmouthshire.

He appeared in 19 of the 26 matches while retaining his enthusiasm and flair for the game, and thoroughly enjoyed his off-the-field activities, developing a high standard of team spirit. His experience in 1969 with the Welsh team served him well and he was acutely aware before the tour started of New Zealands' strength and weaknesses, while his close co-operation with Carwyn James ensured a completely united front to the problems of tactics and selection. Manager Smith dealt with the 'heavies' and the administration, and frequently joined the practices and supplied, with James, a sense of companionship and discipline to the team.

Top New Zealand officials, so long disturbed by the somewhat haphazard manner in which the Four Home Unions selected their officials and prepared their sides, welcomed with open arms, Messrs Smith, James and Dawes, because they were uncomplicated, firm, efficient, friendly, and knew exactly what they wanted to do and where they were going. All three were proud men in a modest and friendly way; but all three were determined; their P.R. work was first-class, and this can be a major feature of any tour, but especially in New Zealand where rugby is not a game but a way of life, where an ankle injury to Colin Meads rates higher in news value than the destiny-deciding terms of the EEC agreement!

Perhaps, their greatest off the field attribute was the fact that they were approachable at all times, and especially by the press, radio and TV, and, as a result, the Lions throughout New Zealand received the maximum amount possible of press comment and quite ninety-nine per cent of it was favourable. I have never found any management unkind or unhelpful to me at any time; this I must say, sincerely, and all have helped make my job much easier, but the top three of the 1971 tour were extremely kind and helpful, and I will cherish their friendships in the game.

The team, naturally, was a happy one and an extremely friendly one, playing and behaving like a club side and this, perhaps, must remain one of the most cheering and successful features of the tour. It was always a pleasure to talk to them and when interviews were required they spoke freely and frankly. They behaved with dignity and decorum and rarely, if ever, engaged in pursuits that caused structural damage and there were no 'wreckers' and 'burners' for, at the slightest suggestion of such an occurence, Manager Smith and Coach James were in with the 'whip' in their own understanding way.

The rules and regulations were few on tour, and after each match, the whole party, together with its accompanying and loyal New Zealand officials, spent three-quarters of an hour together in the team-room, relaxing, singing and joking. This was vitally important, and as match after match was won, the happiness and team spirit at these small parties increased but was never allowed to develop into over-confidence or outward arrogance. On the field there was no show of dispute or disagreement and only the 'King', Barry John, was allowed the full flow of his fancies and amusing antics. The crowd relished the rare occurrence when he was caught – yet all the time they admired his quality, accuracy, skill and indeed, showmanship. It was never arrogance but a genuine love for entertaining and that like a professional, without salary!

Sometimes the party was over-burdened by 'heavies', but this happens in every country and I feel that readers must appreciate that towards the end of any tour for players and camp followers it becomes particularly hard to smile at the right time and always be nice to the right people. This is no reflection upon a magnificently hospitable country like New Zealand or indeed the Lions, for I have found it quite the same when visiting teams near the end of their tours in the British Isles, and there are plenty of 'heavies' in my own country!

I felt this Lions side behaved extremely well; better than most sides even though one has to agree that a winning side is always a happy one, and these Lions created so many records that they were almost bound to be a happy side. In the test series they achieved remarkable results, far greater than anticipated, for they became the first Lions side to win a test series in New Zealand and the first to win a series this century.

In the Provincial matches they were outstanding and became the first Lions side to win all such matches on any one tour this century since Auckland beat the 1904 side. Even if one or two of them were by narrow margins – it may appear a little arrogant for me to say so – never once, after the Wellington match, did I feel that the Lions would lose against a province. That match gave such confidence to the situation that even on the odd occasions that the provinces drew level or the Lions even trailed, one felt they held enough in reserve to pull the match out of the fire. It was this special quality that made them such a fine side. It was this quality that lifted them from being a very good side to a great one.

They loved to attack ... to run with the ball ... to move it from any position on the field ... to counter attack and surprise opponents who had no defence in depth – but they succeeded because they were also great defenders. Rarely, have I seen such cover defence and such remarkable powers of speedy recovery.

It amazed New Zealand watchers to see how the Lions covered each other in defence and were so confident when 'cornered' in any part of the field that if they threw the ball back it would be gathered by a player running into position. In other words, their defensive 'retreats' were always orderly, and there was dignity in their play – even when they were going backwards. Few, if any sides look happy going backwards, but these Lions had the happy knack – or was it skill? – of allowing the opposition to move so far ... and then cut off their support. Whether this was always by design or accident, I know not, but as a defensive system it was superb.

On so many occasions it was written: 'The opposition almost scored'. Much of this was due to the Lions defensive methods and one strategic character was Mike Gibson, whose cover was superb, and another was Barry John. John Williams was a tremendous tackler, stopper and counter attacker. John Dawes always stood firm and kept regrouping his backs, while doing much tackling himself and sharing in attacks. He found added speed on tour and played the best football of his long and colourful career. The wings tackled, too, and their speed of recovery was considerable, for Williams never had to worry when moving up in attack, as he was always well covered.

The real truth is that the side was ORGANISED in front and behind. It knew what to do, when to do it, and how to do, and it had the necessary speed, intelligence and enthusiasm, to be successful at it. All this can be traced to the planning done beforehand by the management. They had studied New Zealand rugby, with James reading everything possible that was written about the game in the Two Islands before the tour, and especially did he read about previous Lions tours abroad and All Blacks tours to other countries, and searched for the reasons why they lost in South Africa in 1970. Among those reasons was hidden the key to success for the 1971 Lions, and here Johaan Claassen was a great help.

James admits that, apart from one or two exceptions, such as a second outside-half to John, since the versatile Gibson was destined to be a test centre and the need of a utility back-come-forward, the selection was a good one for the tour, and all but four of the leading players were available to travel. The party of thirty players and the three replacements mixed extremely well, for they were intelligent, happy, and good mixers and always a unit without any cliques. They were dedicated, more so than any previous touring team, and much of this was due to the attitude of the older players who had made the 'voyage of discovery' before with a Lions side.

Willie John McBride was on his fourth tour and no praise can be too high for his effort as a team man and a worker on the field. He played the best rugby of his career as he trained hard and put the team and the game first at all times. He accepted his responsibility as senior forward, once Ray McLoughlin left, with enthusiasm, and as he knew all the difficulties of touring he was able to get the best out of the younger forwards. It was sad that Ray McLoughlin left when he did, as indeed it was for Carmichael and Hipwell, all victims of the Canterbury Tale, but those who substituted played nobly. Again, those former Lions – Gibson, John, Edwards, Davies, Laidlaw, Pullin, Thomas and Taylor – had all benefited by previous tours and, under 'new management', played extremely well to form nucleus of the side.

Again, it should be emphasised that those Welshmen who had suffered 'humiliation' in 1969, when Wales was routed by New Zealand in two tests... Williams, Davies, Dawes, John, Edwards, Thomas, Davies and Taylor... wanted to achieve 'revenge' for those defeats by playing good rugby; winning some of the tests, and proving to the world that Wales in 1971, when winning the Grand Slam, was a team of talent and dedication. They gave everything they had for the Lions, and as a result, achieved their ambition. The Lions won two of the tests and New Zealand, freely and generously, regarded the once disappointing Welsh as fine players.

Above all else, the 1971 Lions had a desire to do well and the players readily accepted the leadership appointed and the coaching employed, and this encouraged them to produce the best of the skills they possessed. They had ability, and they had strength in depth, and those who did not play in the tests but who supported enthusiastically from the touch-line, are deserving of praise, for every successful side is as good as its reserves. James saw to it that as many players as possible were kept happy and played a many matches as possible and only Biggar failed to reach double figures in appearances, and this was prevented by injury and illness near the end when he missed six matches.

Tactically and technically, the Lions set out first to improve their scrummaging power and succeeded with remarkable results, as outlined in later chapters. Then there was the need to contest every line-out, and spoil and harass as did New Zealand forwards, after first checking with New Zealand referees what was and was not allowed, in the shambles that is called line-out play in the land. Messrs D'Arcy, Kelleher and company would be horrified at the sight of it! Rucking was also important, and as coach James says: 'It was difficult to develop this in training without risk of injury'. Later he argued quite rightly that New Zealand place too much emphasis upon rucking at expense of other phases of play.

The great problem on tour, however, was that of injury and it will remain so. No matter what country is visited, injuries in a game of bodily contact can occur through accident or design, and Lions had their share of both. In Canterbury three players were lost and, surely, that of Carmichael was by design, or how else would he have been so badly injured? Rugby is extremely physical in New Zealand, but these Lions hardened themselves to it and stood up to it remarkably well, yet the four Tests were clean and sporting, if tremendously hard, and this spirit of approach lifted the tour above that of a normal one. It was a great one, and the Lions were magnificent. British rugby owes them much. Well done!

CHAPTER TWO

The Scarlet Runners

It provides much pleasure to pay tribute to the 1971 Lions, collectively and individually. The tour proved successful because it was well-planned and prepared for by the three men who guided it and because they were able to work well together and as individuals. For the first time on a tour there was a clear-cut 'job definition' and, to ensure that all went smoothly, the chairman of the Four Home Unions tours committee, John Tallent, took it upon himself to outline this personally with the three leaders, one week-end, during the tour preparations. Benefiting from lessons of previous tours all three worked in close harmony, although retaining their individuality, and can be classified in rugby history as 'highly successful' in their task. They were experts at rugby football and management.

For Manager DOUGLAS SMITH it was the realisation of an ambition to return to New Zealand and, having failed on two previous occasions to be appointed honorary manager of a Lions side, he was more determined than almost anyone in the party to succeed. He did his job well, extremely well, and if he was fortunate in having such a fine and able party to command, he did give it leadership with the slightly iron hand in the velvet glove. Such an approach is necessary on every tour and, as a medical man, he was better fitted than most to understand the problems that confront young men on tour, on and off the field.

A true Scot, living and working 'in exile' in Essex, he understood the New Zealand approach and retained his sense of humour in public and in private, for managing a touring team is a difficult task; probably the most difficult in rugby administration, especially having charge of a British Lions side. Yet Douglas Smith did it extremely well, twenty-four hours a day, although it was a considerable strain upon his strong and ample frame!

Travelling with him and chatting to him regularly, I found him completely in control of the situation and a team man from first whistle to last. He mothered them, cajoled them, ordered them, coaxed them and sometimes scolded them, and was ever ready to answer just criticism but annoyed at unfair comment – and in certain New Zealand papers there was some right 'rubbish' written! As it was such a successful and happy tour, a small section of the press, but not those travelling with the team, attempted to 'create' controversy which generally destroyed itself through its inaccuracy. One or two of the more lurid items did disturb Manager Smith's equilibrium but he made no comment about them in public and it was indeed hard to get him to comment on Coach Vodanovich's remarkable outburst about 'Passchendaele'. Manager Smith, greatly to his credit, played it cool and with a smile, and his shrewd approach kept the 'show on the road'.

Naturally, he now gains a top place among British managers, alongside Jack Siggins of 1955, because his team was successful. Generally, when things go wrong on tour, folk at home tend to blame the manager but, if things go well, there is praise for the players. It should be said of 1971 that 'Doc' Smith played an important and vital part to earn the respect of his team, New Zealand officials and members of the press.

For the first time in New Zealand the appointed coach was free to coach, and CARWYN JAMES of Cefneithin in West Wales thus became the first man to coach a British team in New Zealand. He made a wonderful job of it. In three months he won the admiration of all New Zealand and one could say that he won his 'battle' with rival coach Ivan Vodanovich 'on points' by achieving what was once thought to have been impossible. Basically, he was successful because he loves rugby football very deeply, and applied his considerable knowledge with the tidy and disciplined mind of a college lecturer plus an extremely pleasant personality.

Perhaps his greatest gift was his sense of diplomacy and his considerable tact in dealing, mainly, with his own players and the travelling press, as well as thousands of callers, the few irritating characters who will persist in 'harassing' players and officials in every country. He shunned no one and because of his determination and ability to get his team to succeed, he was admired both inside and outside the party. Like his manager and his players, he gave up much time to visit hospitals, schools and clubs, and spoke freely about all topics.

He trained hard with his side but still kept his cigarettes going off the field! He confessed to spending sleepless nights on occasions worrying about his team before big matches. He did many broadcasts and made many TV appearances and was often rung early in the morning by BBC (Wales) and asked for comment in Welsh. Outwardly, little appeared to disturb him, but like all Welshmen he is emotional and sensitive, deep down, and he has firm political views, but he never allowed these to emerge to the possible embarrassment of himself, or anyone else, during the tour.

Carwyn James was an ideal coach; a successful one and an excellent tourist, who set a new standard in Lions' team preparation. He was a friend of mine long before the tour was thought of and, naturally, it gave me much pleasure as an onlooker, to see him succeed 13,000 miles from home. Perhaps, I enjoyed his company for two special reasons... his clear thinking and purposeful approach to rugby football and his bubbling, amusing sense of humour.

If James was the first man to coach a Lions side in New Zealand then SIDNEY JOHN DAWES became the first Welshman to captain a full British Lions team, and because he did the job with immense charm, shrewdness, tact and success, he destroyed for all time the myth developed in other countries, that no Welshman would prove good enough to lead the four countries team. At the end of the tour, those who shouted the loudest against a Welsh captain, praised Dawes the most!

Before the tour started, and long before the thirty players were selected, John Dawes was the only real candidate for the job. He had all the necessary qualities for leadership: much experience, and he was an international captain capable of leading Wales to a 'Grand Slam' victory. There just was not another candidate in his class but, strange as it may appear, red herrings were raised in all three other Home Countries and some went like this, 'If a Welshman is captain, the Welsh will run the side, to the exclusion of every one else'...'Dawes may not hold his place and then someone else would have to lead in the tests'...'Welshmen do not make good tourists. Even Terry McLean, writing in *The Times* of London, before the tour started, was in no way complimentary to the Welsh and indicated that previous touring failures were largely the fault of the Welsh!

Thus when Dawes was rightly and unanimously selected, he faced a considerable challenge. He had to break down barriers and prejudices, but he knew that both Douglas Smith and Carwyn James wanted him as captain, and that he was 'their man'. He was also the 'players' man' and by the end of the tour he had proved one of the best Lions captains and certainly the most successful.

He did everything with a gentle smile and his amusing sense of humour twinkled in his eyes but he earned the respect of all by favouring none, and making sure that from the moment the team met at Eastbourne until they returned to London Airport on August 16, tired but happy, that they were a British team. What Dawes did for Welshmen and Welsh rugby, in a quiet way, can never be over-praised, but what he did for the prestige of British rugby was tremendous. He formed, with Manager Smith and Coach James, the happiest, most successful and most efficient partnership in rugby team management ever to leave the British Isles. The players they managed formed a 'happy ship' and I found them extremely likeable, courteous, and friendly, and as good a crew as ever I sailed with in search of rugby!

JOHN PETER RHYS WILLIAMS (London Welsh), full-back. Aged 22. 6 ft. 1 in. 13 st. 8 lb. *Caps:* 16. *Tour appearances:* 15. *Tests:* 4. Medical student.

In New Zealand, where they can judge full-backs accurately and only the brave and brilliant survive in the position, he was rated as the best since Terry Davies of 1959. Indeed they ranked him with Davies, Bassett, Brand and Nepia which was praise indeed. Young, strong and extremely courageous, he was ideally suited to the demands made upon him as an attacking player of rare skill in his position and as a brilliant defender. Whether it was the 'up and under' or the forward drive, William stopped it, and not by brute force alone because he is blessed with a splendid sense of anticipation and a good eye for the moving ball, as befits a fine young tennis player from a truly sporting family. Because of the success enjoyed by Barry John as a place kicker and punter, he was rarely called upon for such kicking duties.

ROBERT HILLER (Harlequins), full-back. Aged 28. 6 ft. 2 in. 13 st. 8 lb. *Caps:* 16. *Tour appearances:* 11. Business representative.

An experienced player and ideal tourist who did not let the side down whenever he played and never complained of his lot after being second choice in the position for the second successive tour. After seeing Kiernan play in all the tests in 1968 he had to watch Williams do the same thing on this tour. This did not deter him from being an excellent team man as he has been for many years for England, Surrey and the Harlequins. He scored in every match in which he played, as did Barry John, and in his 11 matches collected 110 points which was most satisfactory. At Greymouth he gave one of the most accurate displays of straightforward place kicking seen for many years. At first New Zealand crowds got niggly because he took such time and care over his kicks and this was accentuated by the fact that Barry John just put the ball down and swung his leg. Nothing, however deterred Hiller, as the Referee could add what time he felt necessary. As one wag shouted, 'They should have a clock for Hiller!' but he joked his way through the tour, happily, yet hiding a true sense of loyalty and sincerity.

JOHN CHARLES BEVAN (Cardiff College of Ed. & Cardiff), three-quarter. Aged 20. 6 ft. 13 st. *Caps:* 4. *Tour appearances:* 15 *Tests:* 1. P.E. Student.

Made splendid debut for Wales in 1970–71 season and was then popular choice for Lions. At the start of the tour his play was quite sensational and he raced over for try after try to collect 11 in his first five matches but the best of them must be that scored in the closing stages of the Canterbury match – it is doubtful whether any other wing would have achieved it. Young and shy off the field, he was often aggressive on it, but New Zealanders admired the way he went for the line and for the tackle, although sometimes through a lack of experience, he revealed an inability to judge situations. However, he was certainly one of the tour's successes and will play for his country for many years. An expert gymnast, as befits a P.E. student at Cardiff College of Education, he is immensely strong and was a match for all the Lions props for strength!

ALASTAIR GOURLAY BIGGAR (London Scottish), three-quarter. Aged 24. 6 ft. 1½ in. 14 st. 3 lb. *Caps:* 10. *Tour appearances:* 9. Exchange broker.

Although Biggar did not get a test he rendered admirable service to the team and took his chances, readily, whenever he played, as his tally of tries suggests. He was long striding and strong on the left wing and played especially well at Blenheim and Invercargill where he beat defenders on the inside and outside in classical style. Tall and big for a wing, he was unlucky that the tour party contained a few players who were just a shade faster and slightly more elusive. Yet had he played in the tests he would not have let down a side that was suffering from an embarrassment of riches, throughout the tour, at three-quarter. An excellent tourist and a good mixer with his debonair manner, he helped maintain the high standard set by the Scottish 'branch', on and off the field.

THOMAS GERALD REAMES DAVIES (London Welsh), three-quarter. Aged 26. 5 ft. 9 in. 11 st. 8 lb. *Caps:* 17 *Tour appearances:* 10. *Tests:* 4. University student.

Could not join the party until May 30 owing to examinations at Cambridge University, which he passed successfully. He had his first match at Timaru. From that moment he never looked back, proving himself the wing of the tour. Bevan had been the champion before Davies, and Duckham was there to challenge, each in their own way, but the accolade must go to the irrepressible Davies, who bubbled with speed and elusiveness like vintage champagne. His dramatic changes in pace, his sudden side-step, and then the body swerve and jink – he had the lot. His tries at Napier, and in the Second Test must put him in the Ken Jones, Jackson and O'Reilly class as Lions wings in New Zealand. Unassuming, yet enthusiastic at all times, with his captivating smile, Davies was always gentle in appearance, but ran with the speed of the wind and was equally determined. A big success.

DAVID JOHN DUCKHAM (Coventry), three-quarter. Aged 24. 6 ft. 1 in. 14 st. *Caps:* 14. *Tour appearances:* 17. *Tests:* 3. Bank official.

Looked impressive with his flowing blond hair in the slipstream as he raced in for six tries at Greymouth to create a new

Lions' record as an individual try scorer. David Duckham scored some very good tries on tour. At first it was he and John Bevan, but then Davies arrived to become first choice, as loss of form and injury saw Bevan fall away a little. This allowed Duckham and Davies to pair up but there was always the challenge of Bevan for Duckham, although they contrasted considerably in style. The long-striding Duckham was half-centre, half-wing, in his approach but better, I feel, as a wing where he could cover and side tackle rather than engage in frontal tackling. He was the team's accountant and as a bank official kept 'good books' even in the panic of test match days. Invariably, he had pen and paper in hand, either writing home, or checking accounts.

ARTHUR JAMES LEWIS (Ebbw Vale), three-quarter. Aged 27. 5 ft. 10 in. 13 st. 7 lb. *Caps:* 4. *Tour appearances:* 10. Electrician.

Early injury and lack of opportunity later prevented New Zealand seeing the best of this strong Welsh centre. Like Rea, he was in the shadow of Dawes and Gibson, and this remains one of the hazards of touring, for he and Rea would have been played at centre by New Zealand, who lacked a top class player in the position. A strong tackler, Lewis was at his best in the hurly burly of the Canterbury match, where he stood firm in midfield with Dawes and enjoyed every minute of it. A happy tourist, he was entertainments officer and made a success of it in organising birthday arrangments and parties at the hotels. He may not have hit the headlines, but the loyalty of players like Lewis, when not getting enough matches, is vital.

JOHN SOUTHERN SPENCER (Headingley), three-quarter. Aged 23. 6 ft. 1½ in. 14 st. 5 lb. *Caps:* 13. *Tour appearances:* 10. Articled solicitor.

Spencer took a long time to settle to New Zealand conditions and apply his ability. He was strong and determined in his play, and was tried on the wing at first, in the absence of Gerald Davies, but then moved into the centre. Yet it was not until Masterton and then on the wing, that he struck his best form and scored a try in keeping with his English reputation. He did not lack confidence in himself and was a cheerful tourist but did not, unfortunately for him and the side, play as well as he can do, no matter how hard he tried. Like Lewis and Rea, he was unlucky in an over-crowded three-quarter group, although all three were never out of favour and were played when possible.

CHRISTOPHER W. W. REA (West of Scotland), three-quarter. Aged 27. 5 ft. 8 in. 12 st. *Caps:* 13. *Tour appearances:* 10. Broadcasting official.

It was not a lucky tour for this quiet, likeable Scot who could not play his first match until Pukekoe through injury and who, like Arthur Lewis, could not make the test side because Dawes and Gibson were playing so well. Yet he was an extremely loyal tourist and often a brilliantly elusive runner. He had to play at outside half on occasions but was much better at centre. At three-quarter, Lions had too many players and as is inevitable on tour, some players do not get enough regular match play to produce their best. Yet Rea will hold his place in the Scottish XV for several seasons yet. It was nothing to do with ability but merely lack of opportunity that affected Rea, as it did other players in the side.

CAMERON MICHAEL HENDERSON GIBSON (N.I.F.C.), three-quarter. Aged 28. 5 ft. 11 in. 12 st. 5 lb. *Caps:* 35. *Tour appearances:* 16. *Tests:* 4. Solicitor.

Played the best rugby of his long and colourful career on this tour and also proved, by many a moon, that centre is his best position. Between Barry John and John Dawes he was immaculate, running and thrusting, and taking, drawing and giving perfectly and it was a pleasure to watch him. As a critic who felt he was never really happy at outside half I was delighted, as I am sure Michael was himself, that he played so well. His effort, like those of Williams, Dawes and Davies, in producing the first try in the Second Test will remain a happy memory of British back play. Again in the Wellington match, Gibson was outstanding, and as a defender, always he did his stuff as a superb coverer. An excellent. happy, handsome, but often extremely serious tourist.

BARRY JOHN (Cardiff), outside-half. Aged 26. 5 ft. 9 in. 11 st. 11 lb. *Caps:* 22. *Tour appearances:* 17. *Tests:* 4. Finance Executive.

The pages of this book are full of the outstanding achievements on the field of this truly remarkable and amazingly casual and modest young man who, in New Zealand, established himself as one of the great players in his position. Given the accolade of 'The King', unreservedly, by his team colleagues, he was the most talked about, the most fascinating, and the most prolific scoring member of the party. Bush, Spong, Kyle, Morgan and Risman had gone before him with distinction and they formed a parade of champions but John became, in his own special way, as fine and as effective as any of them. An individualist within the side; blessed with the true touch of genius, he never worried about the game or his own play. He was a thorn in the flesh of every defender in New Zealand and a nightmare, ghoulish figure to the 'infringer', as his accurate right boot punished all with round-the-corner instep place kicking.

GARETH OWEN EDWARDS (Cardiff), inside-half. Aged 24. 5 ft. 8 in. 12 st. 7 lb. *Caps:* 23. *Tour appearances:* 16. *Tests:* 4. Management trainee.

The other half of the record-breaking Welsh half back partnership, Edwards had a 'thing' about New Zealand as a result of having to play in two punishing tests for Wales in 1969 when he was far from fit. It took him some time to conquer his own feelings in this matter and do himself justice, as well as recovering from a persistent hamstring injury that has 'dogged' his career. Yet when he was at his best he played magnificently as against the Maoris, Wellington, Otago, Canterbury, Hawkes Bay and Auckland, before putting on a superb display in the Third Test. For much of the tour he was put under pressure unnecessarily, by his forwards tapping back, and by a lack of back row protection at scrum and ruck, as in the Second Test. When positions were reversed for Going and himself, in the Third Test, he proved the match winner, and no scrum-half could have done better than he did in that match. If John was the suave, casual tourist, Edwards was an emotional Welshman who occasionally felt the 'pangs of hireath'.

RAYMOND HOPKINS (Maesteg), inside-half. Aged 25. 5 ft. 8 in. 13 st. *Caps:* 1. *Tour appearances:* 11. *Tests:* 1. Fitter and turner.

One of the two 'funny' members of the party, providing the

traditional easy, open wit of the Welsh Valleys, to complement the sophisticated and quick fire approach of Bob Hiller. Such men are vital for any successful side and Hopkins did an excellent job on and off the field, for he was a scrum worker that impressed New Zealanders and it was good for him and the side that he emerged from the 'shadow' of Gareth Edwards to play with considerable skill and courage in the First Test and share in a unique victory. In the Llynfi Valley, Hopkins is a 'hero' but wears the title modestly and with pride, for his club had achieved big things during the 1970-71 season and his selection for the team capped a winter of content. He burst upon the representative scene for 15 minutes at the end of the England v. Wales match at Twickenham in 1970 after a good 1969 tour in New Zealand and became 'Chico'.

FRANCIS A. L. LAIDLAW (Melrose), hooker. Aged 30. 5 ft. 10 in. 13 st. *Caps:* 32. *Tour appearances:* 11. Sales manager.

A most senior member of the party, making his fourth tour abroad, and proving as effective as ever and an excellent, cheerful, thoughtful tourist. After playing three matches he damaged knee liagments in training and was forced to miss the next six. It was touch and go for some time as to whether he would recover, but the 'wee bitty' man is persistent and returned to play his full part in the tour. He has been Scotland's regular hooker for seven seasons as his tally of 32 caps suggests, and always a quick, clean striker with enthusiasm in the loose plus the traditional durability of a true Border man. Blessed with an excellent voice he enjoyed most of all the tuneful melodies from the *Sound of Music,* and rarely failed to greet those Scottish immigrants of yesteryears still suffering from the call of 'hireath'.

JOHN VIVIAN PULLIN (Bristol). hooker. Aged 29. 5 ft. 11 in. 14 st. *Caps:* 19. *Tour appearances:* 16. *Tests:* 4. Farmer.

A quiet, conscientious, straightforward but skilled hooker. A gentle, pleasant and sincere tourist, who gave not a moment's trouble on or off the field, and was liked by all. A true man of the West Country, with a genuine love of the game, he felt it was his duty to serve it well. Had much work to do on tour as his friend and fellow hooker, Frank Laidlaw, suffered damage to knee ligaments in training and Pullin had six successive matches and a one match break before the First Test. His standard was good throughout although he was the 'target' for illegal punches against Canterbury and Hawkes Bay, and was forced to leave the field at Napier. This never ruffled his dedicated and sporting approach to the game he loves so dearly. Bristol should feel proud of John Pullin.

ALEXANDER BENNETT CARMICHAEL (West of Scotland), prop-forward. Aged 27. 6 ft. 2 in. 15 st. 7 lb. *Caps:* 22. *Tour appearances:* 6. Engineer.

Extremely popular member whose severe facial injuries suffered in the Canterbury match reflected one of the worse moments of a happy tour. Lions lost one corner stone of their powerful scrummaging unit and were fortunate that McLauchlan and Lynch made good the loss of Sandy Carmichael and Ray McLoughlin. Big, strong and fast and one of the world's cleanest and most sporting props, he played in six of the first eleven matches before being injured and would have been first choice at test prop. Was a delightful fellow off the field and was particularly interested in Vivian Jenkins' dog!

JOHN FRANCIS LYNCH (St Mary's College), prop. Aged 28. 6 ft. 15 st. 4 lb. *Caps:* 4. *Tour appearances:* 15. *Tests:* 4. Vintner.

Big, strong, burly Irishman who made Irish XV at late stage in career and fully justified his choice by winning Lions tour place. Was second choice prop at start of tour but when Carmichael and McLoughlin were 'felled' by Canterbury, he filled the breech nobly with McLauchlan and was in the four tests to deserve his share in team victory. Strong and determined, he was an honest, hard working forward on tour. Cheerful and quiet off the field, he occasionally delighted at parties with his traditional Irish singing, and a soulful rendering of *Summer time!*

JOHN 'IAN' MCLAUCHLAN (Jordon Hill College), prop. Aged 29. 5 ft. 14 st. 6 lb. *Caps:* 9. *Tour appearances:* 18. *Tests:* 4. P.E. Instructor.

A magnificent Scot christened the 'Mighty Mouse' by Manager Smith and fully deserved the title. As the shortest post-war Lions prop, he gave mighty displays and was rarely if ever mastered. He could push opponents six inches taller than himself up into

The 1971 British Lions – official team picture. *At back* (l. to r.): C. W. Rea, A. J. Lewis, J. V. Pullin, A. B. Carmichael, J. F. Slattery, J. McLauchlan. *Third row* (l. to r.): J. P. R. Williams, J. F. Lynch, A. G. Biggar, R. Hiller, M. L. Hipwell, D. Duckham, J. C. Bevan, J. R. Taylor. *Second row* (l. to r.): J. S. Spencer, P. J. Dixon, G. L. Brown, T. M. Davies, W. J. McBride, M. G. Roberts, D. L. Quinnell, W. D. Thomas. *Sitting* (l. to r.): G. O. Edwards, F. A. L. Laidlaw, R. J. McLoughlin, Dr. D. W. C. Smith (Hon. Manager), S. J. Dawes (Captain), C. R. James (Hon. Assistant Manager), C. M. H. Gibson, B. John, R. Hopkins. *Absent:* Gerald Davies, G. J. Evans, C. B. Stevens and R. J. Arneil who joined the party after the start of the tour in New Zealand.

The first try in New Zealand. Gareth Edwards about to pounce on the ball in the first match at Pukekohe, as Combined scrum-half W. Cummings fails to gather over his own goal line after a set scrum. BELOW: The Lions' choir at Wanganui. John Taylor leads them in *Sospan Fach* at Wanganui airport. L. to r: John Taylor, Douglas Smith, Chris Rea, Derek Quinnell, John Spencer, Gordon Brown and Carwyn James

the air and was a most difficult man to scrum against. Like Lynch, did notable 'rescue' job for Lions in the test series and smiled his way through every game. On the field he was immensely strong but off it was gentle and engaging character and excellent tourist, relishing an honest talk about front row play.

RAYMOND JOHN MCLOUGHLIN (Blackrock), prop. Aged 31. 5 ft. 10 in. 15 st 5 lb. *Caps:* 22. *Tour appearances:* 5. Chemical engineer.

Biggest blow suffered by Lions during tour was loss of McLoughlin in the Canterbury match, for he was outstanding, tactically, in forward play and the main pack leader. Experienced with long service for Ireland, he had toured the Antipodes in 1966 with a disappointing side and was determined to make 1971 Lions and himself succeed this time. Was halfway to achieving ambition when he damaged thumb during 'retaliation act' in sad Canterbury match. Could have played again on tour, as it turned out, but F.H.U.T.C. had made decision, sent replacement as requested and he had to return. Master scrummager and student of forward play, he was excellent and observant tourist. It was always enjoyable and informative to discuss game with him and one could not but admire his dedication and shrewd brain. Was greatly missed in test series.

BRIAN STEVENS (Harlequins), prop. Aged 29. 5 ft. 11 in. 15 st. 6 lb. *Caps:* 5. *Tour appearances:* 6. Farmer.

Called to duty as replacement when Carmichael and McLoughlin were declared unfit and requested to return. Made first appearance in 14th match of tour and was genuine, hardworking West Country forward, who went near to original selection. Not recognised early enough by England, he achieved fine reputation in Cornish County rugby and recently decided to play for Harlequins. Good tourist and mixer with friendly smile, he was delighted with honour of becoming Lion and like Pullin was interested in New Zealand agriculture and in playing straightforward, honest rugby.

GEOFFREY JOHN EVANS (London Welsh), lock. Aged 28. 6 ft. 4 in. 16 st. 7 lb. *Caps:* 5. *Tour appearances:* 6. Lecturer.

Like Stevens, big Geoff Evans who was unlucky to miss

original selection, came as replacement when Carmichael and McLoughlin returned and proved himself a hard-working lock, well-suited to New Zealand conditions. Had played for Wales in 1970 but then lost place against France in that year and could not regain it from Club and flatmate, Mike Roberts. Good tourist and his Chou Chin Chow moustache set pattern as for 'Mao Sei Tung Seven', as London Welsh members were called. Excellent mixer and thoroughly enjoyed tour on and off the field, in his own quiet way. He was effective in tight and loose play, scoring one fine try against Auckland. Specialised in two-handed catches in short line and Wales should not continue to neglect his skills.

GORDON LAMONT BROWN (West of Scotland), lock. Aged 23. 6 ft. 5 in. 16 st. *Caps:* 11. *Tour appearances:* 14. *Tests:* 2. Bank official.

Youngest and tallest of lock forwards who had had three seasons experience with Scotland and served under his brother Peter, last season's Scottish captain. Good-looking, with engaging smile and soft Scottish accent, he was hard-working forward and one of the most improved in the side, fully deserving his first test cap in third match at Wellington. Used his height well at line-out and although occasionally 'trampled on' in the rucks on the field he enjoyed himself and proved an interested, polite and well-behaved tourist. His one regret was that his older brother, Peter, was not with him to honour a soccer-playing father with two Lions sons!

WILLIAM JOHN MCBRIDE (Ballymena), lock. Aged 31. 6 ft. 3 in. 16 st. 12 lb. *Caps:* 45. *Tour appearances:* 15. *Tests:* 4. Bank official.

The 'big' forward in a 'big' side whose two amusing sayings, 'I hate small men' and 'There are not many of us left', were highlights of the pleasure and joy he obtained from the Lions' First Test victory. He was making his fourth tour and this was his first victory in a test, which he duly celebrated by singing delightfully in Queenstown. Never was honour more deserved, for McBride has served Irish and British rugby extremely well in a long career which began in 1962. In ten seasons a record of 45 caps for his country and four successive Lions' tours is quite remarkable. With his test appearances he is the most capped of

European forwards, ahead of Benoit Dauga, but the greatest tribute that can be paid to him is that he is one of three great locks of his era, sharing the honour with Frick du Preez and Colin Meads. On this tour, easily his best, he was of outstanding value as the hard 'core' of the test pack. He trained hard and played hard, and off the field enjoyed his pipe, a jar, a chat and a song. A man's man who enjoyed every moment of life and had friends everywhere. New Zealanders admired him, and none more than Colin Meads who handed him his jersey in the Lions' dressing room after the match. For me McBride will remain a name, a man, and a friend to remember.

MICHAEL GORDON ROBERTS (London Welsh), lock. Aged 25. 6 ft. 4½ in. 16 st. 12 lb. *Caps:* 4. *Tour appearances:* 11. Accountant.

Won place in side despite close challenge of London Welsh colleague, Geoffrey Evans, because he could play at lock and prop, and prevailing trend was for big props. Said he preferred lock and did not enjoy prop which is understandable for he was hard worker when really fit. He was, virtually, the heaviest forward in the side and had played for U.C.D. and Oxford University before joining London Welsh as partner to Evans, and was recognised for Welsh 'B' side in 1970 before winning four caps in Welsh 'Grand Slam' side in 1971. Admits to having weight trouble unless training regularly he thoroughly enjoyed tour and suffered only one short period of absence through injury.

WILLIAM DELME THOMAS (Llanelli), lock. Aged 28. 6 ft. 2½ in. 15 st. 7 lb. *Caps:* 16. *Tour appearances:* 15. *Tests:* 3. Electrical linesman.

One of the happiest, most likeable and experienced of tourists, making his third trip to New Zealand and, like his friend Willie John, much pleased by the First Test victory which as he said. 'Made all the hard work and effort worthwhile'. A strong, line-out expert, he played his rugby as did R. A. 'Tiny' White, for he always played the ball and not the man! It is true that he often got knocked out of the line-out but he also won a lot of possession. He was honoured as test forward in 1966 before getting first cap for Wales and was doubtful starter for tour with knee trouble but played consistently on tour and was a quiet but happy man. Wrote regularly to home in Carmarthenshire and is said to have received more letters in return than even Tudor James! Was strongly challenged by Gordon Brown after Second Test but always wanted his younger colleague to do well. He had no enemies, in his own or opposing sides, and was much respected. It was his third successive Lions tour.

MICHAEL HIPWELL (Teremure College), flanker. Aged 30. 6 ft. 1 in. 15 st. *Caps:* 11. *Tour appearances:* 6. Army Pilot Officer.

Another casualty of the ill-fated Canterbury match. It is true that Hipwell started his cartilage trouble in New South Wales match but had it 'completed' at Lancaster Park, a ground that held no luck or aid for the Lions in such a pleasant and gentle city! Hipwell first played for Ireland in 1962 and then had to wait another six years before reappearing as a mature player and did well in 1971 season in strong Irish pack. Ideally suited to New Zealand conditions, his departure after playing in six of first eleven matches was a major blow to Lions in tight or loose play off the side of the scrum. A good, cheerful tourist in his quiet way he was desperately disappointed at having to return for an operation when he could have ended tour as one of leading Lions loose forwards.

RODGER JOHN ARNEIL (Leicester), flanker. Aged 27. 6 ft. 3 in. 14 st. 7 lb. *Caps:* 17. *Tour appearances:* 5. Manufacturer.

Came as replacement for Hipwell although was unlucky not to make original selection. Had splendid tour in South Africa in 1968 and played consistently for Scotland at home and abroad. Is big foraging flank forward and enjoyed New Zealand conditions, in country which was last of major rugby countries for him to visit. Extremely pleasant tourist who made friends easily, he had just started in textile business on his own, prior to answering S.O.S. to join Lions. Was with Edinburgh Academicals when first capped for Scotland in 1968 but is now with Leicester, and in 1968 was called into Lions Team on eve of departure as replacement for Bryan West.

DEREK LESLIE QUINNELL (Llanelli), flanker. Aged 22. 6 ft. 3½ in. 15 st. 12 lb. Uncapped. *Tour appearances:* 10. *Tests:* 1. Electrician.

Only uncapped player in side although he had gained Youth cap, played for Welsh 'B' side and for Wales against President's XV, but was popular choice and young player with future after winning and deserving Third Test place. He suffered damaged knee early in tour and after playing six matches missed five before he came back and strongly challenged Kirkpatrick in Poverty Bay match, doing enough to earn Third Test place. Good, foraging, driving forward, Quinnell learned much during tour and was more than useful at end of line-out. A product of youth football, he played for Llanelli for two seasons and was prominent in exciting match against Springboks. Should develop into powerful international forward for Wales.

JOHN FERGUS SLATTERY (U.C. Dublin), flanker. Aged 21. 6 ft. 1 in. 14 st. 4 lb. *Caps:* 4. *Tour appearances:* 13. Student.

Made four appearances for Ireland in 1971 and impressed enough to suggest he would be good developing material, like Quinnell, during tour. By time the Third Test arrived he had made test team but was prevented from playing though illness. Suffered nasty mouth injury in Canterbury match, of unfortunate memory, as result of punch when not expecting it. Good dental surgery plus wearing of plate, on and off field, for long period helped to save some of his loosened teeth. Like most of his countrymen was excellent young tourist and showed fire in loose and ability to drive with ball. Has now completed studies at U.C. Dublin and should serve Ireland well for many seasons as lively successor to Noel Murphy.

JOHN TAYLOR (London Welsh), flanker. Aged 26. 5 ft. 11 in. 13 st. 7 lb. *Caps:* 18. *Tour appearances:* 15. *Tests:* 4. Schoolmaster.

This was his second Lions' tour and second visit to New Zealand where he experienced a hard time with Wales but played tirelessly on this tour for all his lack of inches and pounds. As big 'Little John', he won place in tests and achieved ambition by playing on winning side. Was unlucky with Lions in 1968 in South Africa and suffered persistent knee injury, but enjoyed much better fortune this time. With his flowing hair and beard was christened by his colleagues 'The Man from the Bible,' but was good tourist and extremely quick about the field with excellent hands and sense of position. Was one of seven London Welsh players in side who helped to develop team spirit.

THOMAS MERVYN DAVIES (London Welsh), No. 8. Aged 24. 6 ft. 4½ in. 14 st. 12 lb. *Caps:* 16. *Tour appearances:* 14. *Tests:* 4. Schoolmaster.

An outstanding number eight forward in defence and attack, and one of the most consistent of Lions loose forwards. He had one period of injury lasting five matches as result of kick in lower abdomen, but made excellent recovery to appear in First Test and spell of five successive matches. Tall and slim with an almost delicate appearance that belies his durability, Davies impressed New Zealand critics on tour. Was expert at end of line-out and became more and more of a competitor in this phase of the play following a 'hard' time at hands of New Zealand referees in 1969 with Wales. Davies made sensational entry into Welsh XV as 'unknown' in 1969 and has held his place without difficulty since then. He could follow in line of 'master' No. 8, Alun Pask, with long career in national side. Extremely quiet off the field.

PETER JOHN DIXON (Oxford University), No. 8. Aged 27. 6 ft. 3 in. 15 st. *Caps:* 1. *Tour appearances:* 15. *Tests:* 3. Research student.

Was selected for tour before he had been capped for England and then picked for England in final match of season, following successful appearances for Oxford University and the Barbarians. Fine technical forward who preferred number eight position but also played on flank as result of injuries to others and appeared in three tests as flank forward. Reading for a doctorate at Oxford, he was leading academic of party but extremely courteous and gentle. Was accompanied on tour by his guitar which he played for hours in his room without disturbing the neighbours. A traditional English gentleman, he was an excellent tourist and played conscientiously, but commented after the defensive effort of First Test, 'I had the ball in my hands only twice during the match.' It was as much a moment of glory for him, as for his 14 colleagues.

There were other members of the party who played no small part in keeping the 'show on the road' through the tour. First was *Frank Kilby* of the N.Z.R.U. Council who was liaison officer from start to finish in New Zealand. A retired bank manager, former All Black captain and half back of distinction, he was the successful manager of the 1963–64 All Blacks side in Europe. He was a pleasant character with a keen eye to financial details of touring and kept close hand on over-spending in accordance with N.Z.R.U. decisions. Enjoyed daily visit to the T.A.B. and often 'conferred' with me in the role of imaginary owners as the big races occurred. However, one must report that the occasional 'risk' of fifty cents produced comparatively little profit but when Frank 'put the ring round it', the day was made!

An old friend was baggage master *George Earney,* who remained a good Samaritan to all, and the touring press have reason to be grateful to him. He was rarely 'bridled' and never lost an item of luggage while he coped handsomely with the overweight. He was always immaculately turned out and, in behaviour, a gentlemen, intensely loyal to the Lions party. Only once did I see him annoyed and that was when he was treated other than as a member of the official party by one of the senior unions.

A man who worked really hard to keep the 'show' going was official masseur, former Auckland player, *'Doc' Murdoch.* He was a tremendous enthusiast and a most likeable fellow who would work at any time of day and night to get players fit. He enjoyed a 'party' but his loyalty to the side never wavered even when his own son, All Black Peter, was playing for Auckland against the Lions at first five eighth. One could not but like 'Doc', and it is interesting to think that what Messrs Earney and Murdoch did so efficiently 'in harness', poor Taffy Davies in 1959 had to do alone, and that when he was in his seventies!

The fourth member of the New Zealand section of the Lions party was Alex Macdonald, a quiet former West Coaster and retired civil servant who acted as an efficient secretary to the manager. He, like his three colleagues, had enjoyed much experience with previous tours, and his gentle approach, good humour and helpfulness, played a part in the successful P.R. work carried out by the management.

The touring Press included eight members from the British Isles with six and sometimes five from New Zealand. The home based 'jokers' were Terry McLean (*New Zealand Herald* and any other papers round the world you care to name), Gabe David (*Evening Post* for first half and then stupidly withdrawn but later allowed tests and Saturdays only), Earle Read (N.Z.P.A. and hard working, too, with a pleasant personality), Lindsay Knight (*Dominion* and the man in the 'overcoat' who worked conscientiously for Wellington), John Brooks (*The Press* from Christchurch, quiet, conscientious and a writer of quality and understanding in keeping with best of New Zealand morning papers, *The Press* is occasionally staid but certainly a 'defender of the rugby faith') Bob Irvine (N.Z.B.C. Commentator of many tours) and occasionally others of former tours, like Dudley Manning of Dunedin who does so much good for the *Otago Daily Times* and Larry Sanders of the *Christchurch Star* an experienced journalist who spent so much time, rather unnecessarily I thought, in defending the Canterbury 'stoush'. There were several photographers and they were always helpful and cheerful, with Ian Macklin and Peter Bush as the two 'happy travellers'.

It was essentially a happy press party, for Terry McLean was much mellowed, and more humoured by the even tenor of the tour. An excelllent writer on the game with a deep knowledge and love of it, but his attention was turned, often on tour, to dealing with the 'attacks' of the Auckland Union. He and his paper on one side, and the Auckland Union on the other, were miles apart, but this was a domestic matter that did not concern the casual observer. Mrs Carol McLean and her younger daughter did much to help the Lions with their end-of-tour shopping and this was much appreciated.

Gabe David was always a cheery soul, but greatly disturbed by the extremely unwise act of his paper, in withdrawing him from full-time duty with the tour on 'economy grounds'. An excellent journalist with a friendly approach and a nose for news, he was missed by many, but especially those of us from the 'old country'.

The eight 'gentlemen' from the British Isles were Terry O'Connor (*Daily Mail*), Pat Marshall (*Daily Express*), David Frost (*Guardian*), John Reason (*Daily Telegraph*), Tudor James (*Daily and Sunday Mirror*), Cliff Morgan, Vivian Jenkins and myself. The eight divided themselves, amusingly, into two groups for discussion, namely, the 'Sudaten English' and the 'Welsh Mafia'! It was a happy party with no 'incidents' and the task of covering the tour was made easier by the success of the Lions, the excellent

P.R. work of the management, the friendliness of the players, and the enthusiasm for the tour at home. One can always enjoy working hard when a touring team is successful, and all eight of us enjoyed this tour, more than most, and for me in a purely technical professional manner, it came extremely near to 1955 in South Africa. Indeed, I was pleased to enjoy the privilege of being a member of the 1971 Party and cannot recall having a cross word with any one, for life was pleasant, if often tiring and exacting!

CHAPTER THREE

In the Beginning—Australia

It was a damp and miserable morning when Cliff Morgan drove Tudor James and myself from our hotel to London Airport to set out on yet another Lions' adventure. There had been thunder and lightning during the night, following a long sunny spell, and the atmosphere was heavy. At the airport there were many friends and relations plus a gathering of London Welshmen to see their heroes on to the plane. No one failed to appear and there had been no casualties at the final run-out at Eastbourne, which was a good omen. Manager Smith announced his team for the first match and a 'phone call to home and office 'cast off' the connecting lines and we were away.

Vivian Jenkins had more equipment and luggage than two Lions, including a back scratcher but had forgotten his slippers and shoe trees! He never travels 'light' and his hotel room often looks more like an office on tour. Tudor James and David Frost were the other pressmen with us, as John Reason had gone on ahead to 'buy up' Hong Kong and Terry O'Connor had flown out the other way to miss the Far East, while Cliff Morgan and Pat Marshall were not to join us until mid-June.

The Lions marched out to their BOAC 707 and all shook hands with John Tallent and John Hart, who had done so much, with Phillip Bradforth, to organise the tour. Nine players were touring abroad for the first time, while thirteen of the party had been to New Zealand previously, including five who had travelled with the ill-fated 1966 Lions. At the time of starting the average age of the backs was 25 years and the forwards nearly 27 years and thus it was an experienced side. John Bevan was the youngest player at 20 years and Ray McLoughlin the eldest at 31, while Gordon Brown was the tallest at 6 ft. 5 in. The heaviest back was John Spencer at $14\frac{1}{2}$ stone and the forwards, W. J. McBride and M. G. Roberts, at nearly 17 stone.

One thought of these facts and figures as the 707 flew out over

In the Beginning – Australia

Europe, and wondered what lay ahead for the team, and how all of them would fare on and off the field. The stop at Frankfurt was marked by the refusal of the Germans to allow transit passengers off the plane, followed by another long wait at Rome owing to an Alitalia company strike. The airport was full and they too didn't want transit passengers to leave the plane. It was hot and sticky, with fresh air in short supply. This was no fault of BOAC but one wondered what were the nature of the replies to the questionnaire circulated to passengers on the flight!

Eventually, after stops at Teheran and Delhi, we reached Hong Kong, where I would think it is no easy job to get a 707 on to the causeway landing strip. At the airport John Reason met us with tales of his shopping expeditions in Hong Kong and the purchase of all sorts of things including golf clubs and a telephoto lens for his camera. We reached our hotel, the Hong Kong Hilton, prepared some cables, showered, and then studied the harbour from the 18th floor; at least we counted the number of US ships in the magnificent land-locked harbour which, fortunately, is still a British colony with 10,000 servicemen in residence.

We had flown 7,677 miles from London in $18\frac{1}{2}$ hours flying time, but delays had added nearly five hours and the tight managerial schedule had already taken a stab in the back. Yet Hong Kong proved to be a fascinating place and the local rugby players and officials took those Lions who wanted to go – and it included most of them – on a sight-seeing mission round the City with a strong Chinese flavour! Including the New Territories, the Crown Colony is about 400 square miles but the actual Island of Hong Kong is only 29 square miles. Kai Tak Airport is in Kowloon and the whole place represents a striking contrast between great wealth and desperate poverty, in its population of $3\frac{1}{2}$ millions, many of whom are refugees from Red China.

One of the 'guides' was Dennis Evans, former chairman of Ebbw Vale RFC, an Oxford blue and Welsh international, and another was Paul Gibbs who had toured with the Wallabies in the UK in 1966–67, while Garwyn Young, son of Welsh selector Jack Young, helped the Press party do their shopping. The Lions had a training session at the Hong Kong Club's ground and although the ground was hard the session was quite useful. It was followed by an open air lunch in which several interesting local people were met, including Colonel Norman Roberts of the

Gurkha Regiment. Another was Vernon Roberts (no relation) big business man and rugby official, and he told us that the famous cricket ground was going to be sold in the near future. At such sad news one could almost see Jim Swanton throwing up his hands in horror for it is one of the world's most unusual grounds and certainly the most valuable. Indeed, if you were to own a square yard of ground in Hong Kong, as my wife does in Rotorua, you would be financially blessed!

When we arrived at Hong Kong Airport, ready to leave, it was suddenly discovered that John Bevan had left his passport in the hotel; a search failed to reveal it, which left the manager with several problems but just when he was on the point of ringing London and leaving John 'in transit', another search of the hotel produced it, and the young player flew out with the party. I could not criticise. He was on his first long trip and a few years ago I had left my passport and cheques in Las Palmas Airport while in transit *en route* to South Africa. Fortunately my wife and myself were among the few people to be admitted to South Africa, legally, without a passport. Thus I, at least, can hardly call South Africa a police state!

The journey to Brisbane took us through the night and Manager Smith handed out sleeping tablets to those who required them, but the DC–9 of New Zealand Airways was crammed full, with the seats packed closely together to get as many as possible in, and thus it was not a pleasant journey.

The warm sun of the early dawn at Brisbane made up for everything and although we were all desperately tired, it was good to see Tom McCormick, Charles Blunt and fellow officials, on the tarmac, ready to greet us, together with familar newspapermen like Terry McLean and Gabe David, with newcomer Earle Reed from NZPA. We were soon through customs and immigration and away to an interesting Motel called the Ridge, high above the city, with a delightful all-round view. The sun poured into my room and, as near as one can get to homesickness as a seasoned traveller, my mind went back a few weeks to a pleasant holiday with my wife in Majorca. Travelling is fascinating because of an association of ideas, and time means little, for the whole experience of world travel finds one thinking about so many things in a short period of time.

Unfortunately, there was little time to spare in Australia,

generally, and one could not visit or meet the many friends made during past visits and there was much sleep to catch up on, although I spent that first sunny Monday working on cables, articles and writing letters before retiring to bed a little tired. Barry French, the Australian liaison officer, was most helpful and during the evening the Lions had their first Australian training session under floodlights.

The new Queensland Ground at Ballymore Park, is the first big ground to be owned by a rugby union in the country, and what a fine ground it is, with two other pitches alongside it and a pleasant club house and dining room. One sensed, immediately, the genuine progress made by the Queensland Union and how they were winning their battle against the League Code. Jim Webster and his officials were most hospitable and helpful and Tuesday morning there in the sun was a most pleasant experience, watching the Lions train, surrounded by press photographers and TV cameramen. The tour was really starting and the lunch in the Club house afterwards was most enjoyable and the speeches short but sincere.

First Match
Versus Queensland at Ballymore Park, Brisbane, May 12.
Queensland won by three penalties and two dropped goals (15) to a goal and two penalties (11).
Weather: Dry and warm. *Ground:* Hard. *Crowd:* 11,000. (Record).
Teams:
QUEENSLAND: L. Graham; J. McLean, A. Pope, B. Honan (capt.), R. Miller; G. Richardson, M. Barry; D. Dunworth, M. Freney, B. Brown, S. Gregory, A. Skinner, M. Flynn, K. Bell and R. Kelleher.
BRITISH ISLES: R. B. Hiller; A. G. Biggar, S. J. Dawes (capt.), J. S. Spencer, D. J. Duckham; C. M. H. Gibson, R. Hopkins; J. McLauchlan, F. A. L. Laidlaw, J. F. Lynch, G. L. Brown, W. J. McBride, D. Quinnell, P. J. Dixon, J. F. Slattery.
Referee: Mr Kevin Crowe.

The opening match of any tour is an exciting affair as there is an air of expectation abroad and one sensed this at Ballymore Park in Brisbane on a warm autumn afternoon. Eleven thousand spectators (a record for a Queensland match) were present, and this was twice the size of that anticipated. They were full of optimism that Queensland would win to maintain their good record of recent years. There were tough Queenslanders in their shirt sleeves, many mothers in trouser suits with their young children, and a good many micro-mini-skirted young ladies present, in addition to the large number of local officials and keen all-Australian male sportsmen. It was a day out and a chance for Queenslanders to show the sportsmen from the old country that they were winning the battle against the rugby league, while it was the first visit of the Lions to the new and spacious Ballymore Park in Brisbane, constructed at a cost of nearly £150,000.

There was a presentation from Rothman's towards a coaching course for state rugby and this took place in front of the grandstand before the kick off. It was direct sponsorship but had it happened at Twickenham there would have been an uproar. Quite rightly, Australia and New Zealand do not worry themselves about the outdated regulations and resolutions of the International Board. If any one wishes to present cash for the benefit of the game they accept it and use it wisely, while the four home unions try to remain 'pure' and neglect much-needed cash.

The teams were greeted with cheers, and the Lions started spiritedly but their stamina did not match their enthusiasm and soon they began to feel the joint effects of the long air journey and the heat of the afternoon at 75 degrees. It was too much for the forwards who just could not contain the Queensland pack and this took the fine edge away from the backs, apart from Duckham on the left wing who ran well, and Gibson who covered bravely in defence.

The Lions took the lead in the second minute and held it for 35 minutes but they never really looked like assuming control and winning the match. Hiller kicked a 20-yard goal when Queensland were caught standing up off-side at a maul but for the rest of the half it was Queensland who had the kicks at goal, and they landed two in the last six minutes of the half through Jeffrey McLean their left wing after five failures. In between the two penalties, Lloyd Graham, a full-back with a tremendous punt, dropped a goal and thus it was 9–3 to Queensland at the interval.

The Lions had not gone well enough at forward or behind and the basic errors made cost them valuable points. The forwards could not win the ball at the line-out, were robbed at the mauls, and in trouble in the set scrums, where scrum-half Hopkins and hooker Laidlaw could not satisfy referee Kevin Crowe. Later the referee said that Hopkins was not putting the ball in straight and Laidlaw was kicking through!

In the second half the Lions found that travel fatigue had got them in its stranglehold and, like a cold claw, held them back as they tried to get their second wind. Their speed to the breakdown faded and, however hard they tried, they just could not overcome the handicap. As a result, an efficient, well-drilled Queensland side took charge and relished the opportunity of bidding for success. They appreciated the handicap that the Lions were under, in the hot sun on the hard ground, and they drove in to win the ball at the rucks, with the halves, Barry and Richardson, moving it cleverly.

After 15 minutes they won a five yard scrum and full-back Lloyd Graham was up to take the drop at goal. Over went the ball and it was 12–3 to Queensland; a healthy-looking lead, but a few minutes later the Lions came back into the match to suggest that they would beat off the challenge of the conditions. Hopkins went to the blind side of a maul and was supported by Gibson and Dawes. The Lions' captain got to the line and, as he was tackled, released the ball to Spencer who dived over in the corner. It was a good try, worthy of the Lions, and when the cool Hiller landed a superb conversion from the touch-line to make it 12–8, the interest of British watchers was revived.

Unfortunately, conditions were getting worse at the set scrums, with Hopkins almost afraid to put the ball in and Laidlaw afraid to strike. Each time the Lions got to an attacking position they were penalised and one sensed from the stand that something was wrong for through my glasses I could see a look of frustration on the faces of many players.

After 37 minutes of the second half the Queensland prop 'hooked' in advance and Laidlaw did not strike, but it was a penalty to Queensland for 'not binding'! It was bang in front of the posts and Miller kicked an easy goal to make it 15–8 and victory certain for Queensland. In injury time Hiller landed a fine 42 yard penalty to leave the final score 15–11.

The press gang called Doug Smith out of the dressing room and he was most courteous, despite the disappointment of the moment, and said, 'We have no complaints because of our defeat. I was very impressed by the Queensland side for it was sharp. We started well during the first 20 minutes but then faded and were not sharp enough as well as not taking our chances. Of course, I am disappointed, but we have got it out of our system before going to New Zealand. I have not spoken to the referee and do not intend questioning his decisions. We will abide by his ruling and no complaints will be made by us.'

It was a wise and sensible statement; a diplomatic one, that hid the full sense of disappointment and the confusion among the Lions players as a result of the referee's interpretations. As always, the players enjoyed talking to someone about it, for it had puzzled the press just as much as them, Terry O'Connor blasted away in the *Daily Mail* about appalling refereeing, and most of us quoted the referee as saying, 'I penalised Laidlaw for kicking out and through; Hopkins for not straight; once for a delayed put-in, and once for not binding.'

It appeared that the Queensland scrum on their put-in would give way to the Lions' shove at first and then be called back to the spot of the infringement, whereupon scrum-half Barry would drop it in to the mouth of the tunnel from waist high. It was rather confusing since most of the hooking was done by the Queensland props with their legs often thrashing the air before the ball entered! Hopkins was in trouble from the start and told me, 'Whatever I did, I felt I would be penalised and if it wasn't me it would be Frank Laidlaw! In the end I almost did not want to put it in. It is no use squealing but I have never played in such circumstances before, not even in New Zealand. What with the refereeing and the heat and the travel fatigue, it was hard going! I hope it will be better later on but I felt I was letting the side down.'

Obviously, one did not quote Hopkins then but merely said that he was 'unhappy with his lot'. Kevin Crowe as referee was not directly to blame, perhaps. True, his decisions seemed strange and confusing, but they are always difficult for touring teams in their first matches when abroad. It happens to sides visiting the British Isles, as it does to the Lions, but the whole question is aggravated in the Southern Hemisphere by the constant and unnecessary refusal of the South African, New Zealand and Australian rugby unions to accept neutral referees for test matches.

They are a law unto themselves and, in a way, pay only lip

service to the International Board's regulations, for while a touring team now has a neutral referee for every match in the British Isles, it is a home referee for every match abroad for the Lions. Again, each country interprets the laws of the game as it sees fit and there is no common interpretation, so that unless the Board can achieve this and persuade the Southern Hemisphere countries to have neutral referees the controversy will continue. It is not the fault of individuals but the weakness of the system.

One expected refereeing difficulties even before the match started, but let it be recorded that on the day, Queensland were the better side and well deserved their victory, which was indicative of their growing strength in the game. Queensland are winning the battle against the Rugby League and as the game in the schools gathers momentum it must give great joy to pioneers like Tom McCormick and Jim Webster, and all those at Ballymore Park. There was no bitterness when the Lions left on Thursday for Sydney, and the press conference at the Ridge Motel before we flew out was marked by an amusing determination on the part of Terry McLean to persuade Doug Smith to criticise the referee. It was 'no go' for the Manager was 'politely' on his guard!

The Australian press reports of the match gave quite a bit of stick to the Lions saying they were disappointing. Norman Tasker in the *Sydney Sun* said 'Lions will need a massive lift in forward fire-power if they are to cope with the NSW challenge on Saturday. The Lions turned in one of the softest forward performances Brisbane has seen from a rugby touring team.' Australian papers do not give big coverage to rugby union football but the Queensland match was given more, before and after, than in recent years which is another indication of the union game's increasing popularity.

The management discussed the game freely with me and, while disappointed, realised that there were circumstances beyond their control and the worst of these was the committal by the four home unions of the team to play a match against a strong state XV, only 40 hours after arrival. Manager Smith said that the players were suffering from 'circadian dysrhythmia' or a change of metabolism caused by travel fatigue and that it would take several days to recover from it. It was not an excuse for defeat, as Queensland deserved their win, but a reason for the Lions failure to maintain their good start.

The Ridge Motel at Brisbane was a pleasant place and the weather perfect, although too warm for British rugby men. It was early winter and magnificently healthy, but one realised that it must be pretty hot in summer. Consequently, one felt more than a little sympathy for the recent MCC players struggling in the heat. Again, Queensland folk are hospitable and Greater Brisbane covers 375 square miles to remain the second largest city in the world, although its population is only 700,000. It is well laid out, and bright and clean, and growing apace. Brisbane became a City in 1902 and is one of the 'big five' in Australia as well as an ideal place for a winter holiday.

The flight down to Sydney was quite pleasant and there was a good gathering to greet the Lions at Mascot Airport in warm sunshine, headed by Arthur Henry and Charles Blunt, with Freddie Stovin-Bradford and Bo Stribling, the new secretary of the Australian Rugby Union, and other old friends. Freddie is now president of the Australian Barbarians and a former captain in the Royal Navy, for whom he played at full-back. Now in business in Sydney he enjoys Australia. Arthur Henry, who has done a great deal of work for rugby, had recently returned from London as one of Australia's two International Board representatives.

The Lions had a work-out at Sydney Oval No. 2 ground during the day and were entertained by the Australian Union at the Eastern Suburbs Club during the evening. Wylie Breckenridge was there; a big man and an outstanding figure in rugby football since 1927 when he and his close friend Jock Blackwood were popular Waratahs. It is good to meet former players who have toured in the British Isles for several reasons and, not least, is their ready desire to defend the Lions and to return the hospitality they must have enjoyed in their playing days.

The game owes Breck and the Australian Union much for their persistence in getting the 'no kick to touch' law approved and accepted. It has done so much to improve the flow of the game and reduce touch kicking and while it took many years to get the Board to accept it, it is an excellent change but, to get other equally important changes accepted, we must be patient.

On Friday evening we were the guests of John Attwill at the New South Wales Club with Alan Evans, Sir Dan Ayrons and officials of the Liberal party. It was most pleasant. The NSW Club has amalgamated with the Australian Club, where many pleasant hours have been spent on previous tours.

On Saturday it simply poured with rain and the prospects of a fast-moving, running match were cast aside from early dawn. The forecast for the day was not good and even though one local paper suggested that the rain would favour the Lions it was not true because Lions sides have always played best in good conditions. They wanted to win and were determined to do so. There were several teams talks in Sydney and the side, with ten Welshmen in it, could not be excused on the grounds of a lack of combination and team spirit!

Vivian drove Tudor and myself to the ground through the worst traffic jam I have ever experienced abroad. It took us over an hour to travel two miles. There are three grounds close together in Sydney, the Sports, the Oval and the Showground, and all three were in use at the same time! There was a snarl up and it required much patience, sitting there in the rain, while the traffic stood still. It is recorded that Vivian smoked a few cigarettes during the hour but we got into the Press seats with 15 minutes to spare. A 'curtain raiser' was in progress and this cut up the ground, especially the cricket square in the centre of the pitch, and when the teams fielded to be introduced to the Governor, Sir Roden Cutler, V.C., it rained extra hard.

Second Match
Versus New South Wales at Sydney Oval, May 15.
Lions won by a goal, two penalties and a try (14) to four penalties (12).
Weather: Raining heavily. *Ground:* Very wet. *Crowd:* 22,568.
Teams:
NEW SOUTH WALES: A. McGill; J. Cole, G. Shaw, S. Knight, R. Batterham; T. Stegman, J. Hipwell; J. Howard, P. Horton, R. Prosser, O. Butler, T. Gelling, P. Sullivan, P. Dawson and G. Davis (capt.). R. Smith substituted for P. Dawson in second half.
BRITISH ISLES: J. P. R. Williams; D. J. Duckham, S. J. Dawes (capt.), A. J. Lewis, J. C. Bevan; B. John, G. O. Edwards; R. J. McLoughlin, J. V. Pullin, A. B. Carmichael, M. G. Roberts, W. D. Thomas, J. Taylor, T. M. Davies, M. L. Hipwell.
Referee: Mr C. Ferguson.

One sensed from the start that the Lions would make a special effort and they did so with the forwards driving through, seeking possession, and the halves probing, while one kick, wide of full-back McGill by John, gave Bevan an opportunity to chase and tackle. In such conditions the diagonal kick, the high punt and the grub kick through, were the order of the day.

After 12 minutes the Lions took the lead in the same manner as at Brisbane with a penalty goal, and this time it was Barry John with a kick from 25 yards, to record his first points of the tour. Three minutes later the Lions went further ahead when Barry John kicked from a line-out and Bevan chased to hack on but was half-obstructed. However, Dawes came through really quickly to boot through again, over the line, and beat McGill for the touch down and his first points of the tour. John kicked the goal and the Lions were eight points in the lead after 15 minutes.

However, the Waratahs, as New South Wales have been called for 50 years, steadied and there followed a series of penalty attempts, two by each side. John Taylor and Barry John were wide for the Lions but McGill landed one of his to make it 8–3. In injury time before the interval, a high attacking punt gave the Lions the drive to surge into the NSW '25' where there was a maul, from which Dawes fed Bevan. The pass was forward, because Bevan was slightly in front of Dawes, but the referee was unsighted on the other side of the maul, and Bevan dashed over for the second Lions' try. This, in the end, was to prove the decisive score, and one couldn't knock referee Craig Ferguson for that!

This left the score at 11–3 at the interval with the Lions deserving of their eight points lead. They had played much better than at Brisbane; won more ball and used it wisely behind, with Edwards playing shrewdly and 'shielding' John at outside-half, where he was subjected to stern marking. The pack won more of the ball than at Brisbane and although their rucking was criticised later, there was an improvement. Ray McLoughlin was a sound leader with another Irishman, Mick Hipwell, doing noble work in the loose as a 'pursuer of the leather' – New Zealand style!

The second half became a jolly round of penalty kicks, probably many of them deserved but some not, although it is always difficult to tell at Sydney Oval from the press box, deep over 'third man's head'. Most of the penalties went the way of

NSW and this helped to keep them in the match but it was Barry John who put the Lions further ahead after six minutes. It was an excellent goal from 40 yards and a wide angle, kicked off a soaking wet pitch with a water-logged ball, and he will not kick many better ones!

Immediately, McGill came back with one for NSW from 30 yards and then another after 20 minutes, again from 30 yards, made it 14–9, and extremely interesting. Eight penalties to the NSW side in the second period and one to the Lions reveals the story of the half and, as Edwards chose to play it tighter in the conditions to cut down errors, it became a hard struggle in front. The Lions did not wilt this time as the Waratahs drove through with spirit, and Dawes, Williams and Bevan made several good diving saves.

After 31 minutes McGill took his sixth shot at penalty goal, this time from 25 yards and straight, after Roberts had got a foot in front of the ball at a maul. It was an easy kick and an easy goal but it made the score 14–12 and promised a cliff-hanging finish for the evening papers. Sixteen minutes were to elapse before the final whistle was sounded or rather the hooter, which meant seven minutes of injury time but the Lions survived, even though McGill had one more shot at goal from 40 yards and kicked wide.

One could hear the Lions sigh with relief and, as John Dawes commented with shrewd understatement, 'We were anxious but not worried in the closing stages!' Eventually, the match ended 96 minutes after it started and the Lions were highly pleased at winning after a far more positive display. It had been a strong NSW side including ten internationals and the Lions survived the anticipated barrage of penalty kicks which were awarded mainly as a result of the difference in interpretation. It starts and ends there and the problem is far from settled.

After the match it was good to talk rugby and cricket with such famous cricketers as Alan Davidson, Richie Benaud and others, before Arthur Henry shepherded the press into the NSW dressing rooms for a 'shout'. There was champagne there, too, and one appreciated the hospitality. The friendly 'gang' of Australian 'allikadoos' – Breck, Henry, Blunt, French, McCormick, Eastes and company saw to it that we were happy and there was good spirit in the room during the short after-match speeches.

Both sides thanked Referee Ferguson and no one made any comment on the penalty awards; 19 to NSW and five to the Lions.

The management were pleased with the performance as it was such an improvement upon Brisbane, mainly because the players were getting over their 'circadian dysrhythmia' or travel fatigue, while James' coaching approach was beginning to get through. The forwards worked much harder; produced a strong shove in the set scrums with Ray McLoughlin the corner stone, and dominated the line-out. In the loose they were matched by NSW but Mick Hipwell moved rapidly about the field and in winning so much more ball for their backs, one believes that the Lions' margin of victory would have been greater on a dry day.

In the backs one was impressed by the shrewdness of Edwards in dictating the game tactically; the ability of John to score points in all conditions; the captaincy and soundness of John Dawes and the potential of young Bevan. The ball did not go the way of Duckham on the right wing except in defence.

The Australian press were favourably disposed towards the Lions in their reports and Jim Webster said, 'The tourists adapted themselves so well to the nasty conditions.' Phil Tressidder in the *Sunday Telegraph* wrote, 'The Lions showed their mastery of wet weather football when they triumphed over New South Wales.'

The New Zealand press trio were suitably impressed but still pursued the referee angle and hoped that Manager Smith would utter some words of criticism but, no, the management remained silent. They went with their team to the NSW Rugby Ball after Doug Smith had chatted with me for the BBC in London. He was a happy man!

CHAPTER FOUR

First Taste of the North Island

The last morning in Sydney was spent completing cables, writing letters and packing, followed by a farewell drink with local officials before driving by taxi along the new motor way to Mascot airport. It was beautiful weather and we regretted that our stay in Australia had not been longer, for the early winter sunshine in that country provides the near perfect climate for visiting British folk. At the airport the Welsh press 'trio' decided to bid farewell in champagne and the sight of Frank Cooper, the former secretary of the Australian Rugby Union, was enough to set the party going. Unfortunately, as we started the time honoured toast, 'Here's to rugby men everywhere!' Douglas Smith, fresh from the Motel, told me that my large travelling case had been left behind. Dave Dark, king of Australian baggage masters for many years, had been deceived and the bag was still a long way from the airport with the minutes ticking by. However help was at hand!

Liaison officer Tom Speight and former Wallaby, Abe Hodgson, got to work on the phone and as a result a taxi collected the missing case and the time of boarding was delayed for a dual purpose. First to enable the Lions to have a farewell drink in Aussie and secondly to allow the bag time enough to pass through airport control. One has to be prepared for all sorts of things on a long tour and the only wise approach is not to panic, for there are always friends who will help – one cannot tour without good friends at the various places. The real difficulty is that after several tours one makes so many friends that it is impossible to spend enough time with all of them.

Once on the plane, all was well, and we bade a sad farewell to Australia, after a hurried trip with two hard matches that had provided the Lions with sterner opposition than they had reason to expect. However, the object of the exercise and late agreement to visit Australia was to 'jack up' interest there before the arrival of the Springboks, and put some cash into the coffers.

The 'mission' was successful, judging by the smile on the face of Rugby president, Charles Blunt, as we left, and there was a strong desire on the part of the Australians to have a ten or twelve match British Lions tour in the near future but, at all costs, they needed a continuation of the individual home country tours. The Springboks tour promised them some worry with the threats of demonstrations and the like, but one felt they were determined to preserve the right to play against whom they wished, at all times.

The DC-8 of Air New Zealand was again cramped, although the food and wine was up to standard and the meal much enjoyed. There was a rugby atmosphere in the plane suggesting that we were flying into the 'never, never land' – the land where so few, if any, visiting teams succeed! At that moment, between Sydney and Auckland, I realised how remarkable had been the achievement of the 1937 Springboks in winning the series in New Zealand. They must have been an outstanding, tenacious and clever side.

In the plane were 30 young British players and two managers, bent on achieving success and apart from omissions like Janion and Arneil, and certain players who could not travel, it was the strongest side that could be sent on the mission to overcome New Zealand rugby in its own home, a task never achieved previously by a British side.

The plane touched down in Auckland just after 10 p.m. and as the airport is some way out of the city there was no great crowd of enthusiasts but plenty of officials. They were pleased to see the Lions and the necessary formalities did not take long. After TV and radio interviews given by the management and captain, the Lions and their press party were on their way to the Royal International Hotel in the centre of the city. There were letters from home; an essential feature of touring life, and soon it was bed time, for the long sleep so necessary after a long flight, but this was the last long flight for three months, and what faced the Lions was hard training and even harder matches.

The real atmosphere of a rugby country hit one on landing and there was much talk about the All Blacks final trial which had been held in Auckland on the Saturday. The Sunday papers were full of praise for the powerful rucking and stern forward work and the propaganda machine was in top gear, churning out thousands of words. It makes for enjoyable reading for rugby followers, perhaps, but in New Zealand there is no shortage of newsprint. Before the end of the tour many millions of words would be typed and cabled by all the writers, from the various hotels and grounds.

Frank Kilby, a well-known New Zealand rugby figure, had been appointed NZRU liaison officer and this appeared a good choice as Frank had managed the successful 1963–64 side in Europe and knew the ways of the British in the game. When I asked him about the Final Trial and Colin Meads he made the comment, 'Old pinetree is still thieving as well as ever', which meant that he was still 'stealing' the ball at the line-out! The forwards must have looked good but there was doubt about the midfield backs, and the Lions hoped they would be strong behind, yet it was, in the main, forwards who won the matches, especially in New Zealand.

Doug Smith said on arrival, with a smile on his face, 'I think we can win the test series by two matches to one and one drawn!' and Meads replied, 'I feel the Lions are too cocky!' The battle of words was on, in much the same manner as the Maoris used to make faces at each other years ago, before going into battle. News reached us from Sydney that Referee Ferguson had criticised the Lions after Saturday's match but they remained unperturbed and engaged in the first training session at the Eden Park No. 2 Ground before several hundred spectators. I looked across at the main ground and its fine stands and said to my press colleagues, 'I think I will lay a wreath there tomorrow in memory of Welsh hopes that were dashed on this ground in 1969!'

The next day the Lions trained at Papakura and there was a scare for the side when, accidentally, Duckham put his fingers into John Williams' eyes when attempting a hand off. However, after suffering double vision for a while Williams recovered and resumed training. Throughout the training sessions during the first week in Auckland, James employed variations and never had the two same XV's, or one 15 and one 14 in action, on the same day, in order that players should become acquainted with each other. During one session, James had one line of forwards jumping against another, and he made them move across the line as a body into one another as do the New Zealand packs, and the result was amusing, not to say confusing! It brought home the remark of Gabe David when he said, 'New Zealanders are the world's greatest obstructionists at the line-out!'

Judge Willie John McBride, the 'hanging' judge, held his court at Auckland and fined several players for 'misdemeanours' to further improve the team spirit. News was received, too, that the referees for the first five matches had been chosen and they included the controversial J. P. Murphy, who had done more tests for New Zealand than any other referee. One always laughs when realising that even in this advanced stage in the game's history there are still home referees doing test matches in the Southern hemisphere. Imagine a Wellington referee doing a Ranfurly Shield challenge match at Wellington, between Wellington, and Canterbury! It just would not be allowed, yet the NZRU will not agree to neutral referees for test matches.

In one practice during the week, Spencer clashed with McBride in a tackle and injured his shoulder tnd Arthur Lewis suffered a knee injury while Edwards had to spend a day in bed with a sore throat. As Doug Smith was a medical practitioner he was able to examine all the players first and had a good supply of 'cures for all ills'. Early on the Thursday morning the fire alarm bells rang at the Lions' hotel and while it did not wake everyone, baggage master George Earney was up and down the corridors banging on the doors, shouting 'fire alarm!'

The first Lion to reach the foyer was Mike Gibson, later to be 'charged' by hanging judge McBride for 'deserting the team' but several slept on, including the manager, while Duckham's comment was, 'let me know if there are any developments!' Vivian, Tudor and myself descended with George Earney to the ground floor in comfort via the lift, quite the wrong thing to do, but George Earney had 'tested for smoke'. It proved to be a false alarm due to an electrical fault but rather disturbing, and there were a few weary-eyed characters in the morning.

The team to play in the first match at Pukekohe against the Combined side was announced, and it was a mixture of the two sides that had played in Australia, with seven from Brisbane and seven from Sydney plus Chris Rea who would be making his first appearance of the tour. Williams was at full-back, Spencer and Duckham on the wing, John and Edwards at half-back, and Gibson in the centre with Rea to give Dawes a rest after his two matches in Australia.

This side trained with the other players at Pukekohe on the Thursday and enjoyed the outing to the market garden area of

New Zealand. Situated 32 miles to the south of Auckland, it was a friendly town of 7,000 inhabitants. Its ground was a new one, constructed in amphitheatre of volcanic soil, and its lush green grass glistened in the morning sun as the players entertained almost a thousand spectators. Where else in the world would you expect to see a seventh of a town's population watching a rugby practice? Counties' secretary R. S. 'Bob' Otter was the most helpful of all the many helpful provincial secretaries, while veteran president, the tall broad-shouldered former forward, B. A. 'Ben' Keary, was the gentlest of presidents. All the officials at Pukekohe were pleasant and helpful and proud to be the first side to oppose the Lions in New Zealand. Yet all regretted that the NZRU Council would not allow the Lions to stay in the lovely town. It would have done them a power of good!

Pukekohe farmers grow three crops of potatoes a year and nearly all of them are 'Arran Chief' which are ideally suited to the conditions, while onions are another speciality. Opposite the rugby ground was a small vineyard, one of the few in New Zealand, and the sun shone down from a cloudless sky. How lovely, and a happy memory for all.

In contrast Auckland is a big city, without the sophistication and dramatic pace of modern cities. Fortunately, it has no tension in its atmosphere and black and white mix freely. As one NZ journalist told me, 'We have our problems,' but nowhere in the world does black and white mix as freely as in New Zealand, and one could not help but be impressed by this while walking three times a day to the post and cable office, down the length of Queen Street. The people all looked happy but the Pakehas (white) very much alike, and straight out of a provincial British town, until one spoke to them and the accent, not as hard as that of an Australian, reminded one that it was New Zealand.

One had to get used again to the monetary system which is easier than the new one in the UK, because New Zealand was brave enough to make the main unit the dollar, valued at ten shillings. In the UK we did not want to move away from the £1 but New Zealand agreed to 100 cents per one dollar, the equivalent of the original ten shilling note. Then follows, one, two, five, ten and twenty dollar notes. Having gone from Britain, to Majorca, then back to Britain, followed by Hong Kong, Australia and New

Zealand, in less than three weeks, I accumulated quite a lot of loose change in foreign coins!

On Thursday evening the Lions experienced their first case of petty theft by a sneak thief and the 'victim' was Barry John. He had left the key in his hotel room door for room mate John Pullin to get in, while John was taking a bath. He heard someone entering the room but the intruder did not answer, so John got out of the bath and looked into the room. The door was open and John's camera and watch had disappeared.

However, there was a sequel to this incident, which had disturbed John considerably as his wife has given him the watch as a present and it had much sentimental value. On Saturday evening when the Lions party returned from Pukekohe, baggage master George Earney saw a suspicious character moving along the corridors outside the players' rooms. He informed the hotel manager and the man was apprehended and later charged. It is a feature of touring teams that their hotel rooms are often entered by 'sneak thieves' and the items generally stolen are cameras, watches, pens, jerseys and money.

The Friday before the Pukekohe match was a rest day but Vivian and myself had pleasure in meeting members of the NZRU Council following a meeting. They were in cheerful mood and it was good to see Ces Blazey, Jack Griffiths, Charlie Saxton, Noel Stanley, Morrie Ingpen, Duncan Ross, 'Wild Bill' Craddock and company, and the new secretary, Ray Morgan, who appeared happy and efficient, looking after the 'mourners' as we call them in Wales!

Saturday morning dawned beautifully and Vivian suggested a picnic lunch for the Welsh press trio with an early ride to Pukekohe to get a 'good place' in the car park. It was a pleasant drive out of Auckland, along the newly constructed motorway which is a boon to drivers moving south from the city. As we moved along in a Ford Zodiac (by kind permission of Sam Rees) we appreciated how much per head it must cost the three million population of New Zealand to maintain their roads, since the country is such a big one for a small population. However, the roads are good, better than many young Kiwi drivers, who on Friday and Saturday nights play 'chicken' up to the traffic lights, deserve. Cars are expensive in the country and there are more old 'bangers' per head of population than in any other English-speaking country. Again, many would like to buy British cars but import of them is restricted and they are not always as good a buy as they used to be, which is a sad reflection on British workmanship.

Third Match
Versus Combined Counties and Thames Valley at Pukekohe Stadium, May 22.
Lions won by two goals, three penalties, one dropped goal and one try (25) to one penalty (3).
Weather: Warm and sunny. *Ground:* Dry, long grass. *Crowd:* 25,000 (record).
Teams:
COMBINED XV: R. N. Lendrum; P. Yates, A. Duggan, B. McCollum, M. G. Davis; E. S. McRobbie, W. Cummings; F. T. Richards, B. Cochrane, J. Hodge (capt), R. Clarke, K. Hamilton, S. Tolutu, G. G. Walters, B. Shirkey.
BRITISH ISLES: J. P. R. Williams; J. S. Spencer, C. M. H. Gibson (capt), C. W. W. Rea, A. G. Biggar; B. John, G. O. Edwards; R. J. McLoughlin, F. A. L. Laidlaw, A. B. Carmichael, G. L. Brown, W. D. Thomas, D. Quinnell, P. J. Dixon, J. Taylor.
Referee: Mr L. Gibson (Poverty Bay).

I shared the NZBC commentary with Bob Irvine during the match and at midday, before the picnic lunch in the sunshine, we did a preview. I said that it was necessary for the Lions to win, and win well, for a good start to be made to their tour in New Zealand. Nothing else would do, and as the NZRU Council, selectors and press were present, it was vital to create a good first impression. The ground filled steadily and there was a curtain raiser before the big match between the Juniors of the Counties and their rivals from the Thames Valley and the one feature that struck me was the number of players with long hair, wearing headbands of black plastic! The ways of Europe, for better for worse, had reached New Zealand and maybe, in time, their forwards will prove no harder than those in the British Isles.

Ray McLoughlin was passed fit to play before the match and Barry John's neck injury which he sustained while washing in the morning was not revealed, wisely, by Coach James, although it caused us to think that he had been injured early in the match, as in the press box we did not appreciate the fact that he was suffering pain when passing the ball. In the opening minutes John slipped several times and fell to ground, as he side stepped to set himself up for a drop kick at goal. There was something wrong with his studs!

He was wearing his favourite pair of boots with the studs rather worn and in the long, lush green grass he found difficulty in keeping his feet. This handicap plus his cricked neck, made it difficult for him in the opening stages and many chances were wasted as the Lions pack settled in to win good possession. The scrum packed low and solid to develop a good shove and this surprised many of the experts present. Again, Brown and Thomas jumped well at the line-out and the whole eight did better at the rucks than anticipated. However, it was 20 minutes before the Lions took the lead following a long period of attack.

The second penalty of the match, and the first for the Lions, saw Barry John kick a lovely 30 yard goal from a wide angle and four minutes later he dropped a 15 yard goal, when the ball went back to him from a ruck, following a good back movement that had been held up outside the Combined line. Then John kicked an even better penalty goal from 40 yards and from 0–0 the Lions went to 9–0 in six minutes to take charge of the match. Once again, as at Sydney, John was the harvester of valuable points as he had been all season for Wales in the championship.

Before the interval Edwards scored the Lions' first try in New Zealand and it was the result of sharp pursuit of the ball moving through the Combined scrum, which shot out quickly and Cummings the Combined half-back could not gather it. Edwards dived on the rolling ball to get a finger tip touchdown and Referee Gibson awarded the try. It was not far from the posts but John's kick at goal sailed wide. The Counties countered for a while before the interval but the Lions stood firm and led by 12–0 when play was resumed in the second half.

For a period the play was scrappy and the Lions backs did not function smoothly or produce enough speed on the wings, while the Combined side tackled sternly and were ready with the quick counter. Indeed, there were 18 minutes of play before the Lions added to their lead and then Barry John landed his third penalty goal from 30 yards.

The Counties replied with a good 30 yard penalty goal by McCollum which produced a loud cheer from a sporting crowd, only for the Lions to reply with their best combined try. They moved to the left from a line-out and John Williams entered the line to give Biggar the overlap. The young Scot ran hard before sending inside again to the supporting Williams who put Taylor over for a traditional Lions try. John kicked the goal and it was 20–3 to the tourists. Could they really build up a big score and finish in a blaze of glory?

The Lions' forwards were going well; the front row men were packing low; the line-out men jumping high, and the back row men were quick to the scene of the break down. The halves were not quite as smooth as normally but Edwards frequently sent out his long pass from the set pieces, which enabled the backs to get Spencer moving on the right wing. However, hard though he tried, he could not get clear to score and three times he was stopped in the Combined '25'.

This was due entirely to the fact that he was a centre playing on the wing and coach James admitted afterwards that it was an experiment in the absence of Gerald Davies and that it might not be repeated. Spencer did not have the elusiveness to evade full-back Lendrum and was three times tackled. He lacked a wing's true pace to get outside the full-back, yet he tried hard as did Biggar on the left wing. However, another try was achieved and a good one, highlighting the potential of the Lions, for they moved left and when the movement was stopped, rucked the ball and moved right. Seeing his centres covered, Barry John placed a lovely short diagonal punt over the Combined back line away from Lendrum, and Spencer was able to gallop up and take the ball on the full to score. John kicked the goal and it was 25–3. That was the final score and immediately after the match Manager Smith commented, 'I am very pleased with the result. I thought the forwards did everything that was asked of them, but the backs wasted too many chances. I was very pleased with the refereeing and feel we have made a good start.'

This was a sound assessment of the Lions approach and later in the evening, back at Auckland, members of the NZRU Council agreed with it. The Lions forwards surprised many people in that they revealed the coaching they had received in recent years to suggest they would be a better proposition than the 1966 side. They went into the rucks low and moved over the ball, instead of attempting to rake it back. They did well at the line-out and jumped high, although the NZRU chairman of selectors and coach Ivan Vodanovitch was not happy about the Lions palming the ball down with the outside arm. Immediately, International Board representative Ces Blazey corrected him and pointed out that it was quite legal and that Referee Gibson was correct.

I pointed out to some members that Gibson was a more than adequate referee and could be put on the panel of four referees for the tests, but they argued that he was not in the first six top referees. I then put the case that if Pat Murphy was put on the panel of four it was possible he would not get a test match, which was not well received, although I said most of the party would give a chance to Messrs Pring, Taylor and Miller, unless we saw someone much better. It was a series in which the Lions could take no chances and had to have confidence in the quality of the refereeing. Vivian and myself emphasised to the council members that all the difficulties could be overcome by the appointment of neutral referees.

Vivian's comment was: 'How would New Zealand like to play Wales at Cardiff under a Welsh referee?' This is the true test and as the Lions had been happy with Mr Gibson, who had proved most competent and allowed the advantage law to operate to the full, it is difficult to see why Council members did not rate him. The spirit of the match was excellent and there was only a minor outburst when Quinnell and Shirkey on the flank exchanged a 'Souvenirs' with honours even, and perhaps it was good that what was received was also returned, for it indicated that the Lions were not prepared to play like lambs, but like real Lions!

On Sunday, after an evening of chatter and celebration at Auckland with door banging but no door or glass breaking (South Africa please note), one could reflect upon the Lions' first match and victory as not as good a display as that of 1959 but certainly much better than that of 1966. In fairness, however it must be said that Southland in 1966 were a far stronger side than the Counties in 1971. Again, the change of climate from Brisbane to Invercargill was something to be experienced, blow hot, blow cold, and it did affect the 1966 Lions. Indeed, I do not think, on reflection, that the 1966 side ever recovered from their first defeat by Southland, as it revealed the awful truth of their several weaknesses.

Pukekohe was the reverse, for it gave hope to the 1971 Lions and

ABOVE: One of the biggest welcomes of the tour was received at Wanganui where 5,000 people turned out on Sunday afternoon to greet the Lions and drive them three miles to their hotel in vintage cars. In the leading car are Manager Smith, Captain Dawes and Coach James. BELOW: An important try for the tourists: The Lions' pack leader Ray McLoughlin, crashes over for his try just before the interval at Hamilton against Waikato to increase the lead to 14–8, after the home team had just failed to draw level

The flying Welshman, John Bevan, races past full-back Pickrang to score the first of his three fine tries against Waikato

pointed out that there was a chance for them in the series ahead if they improved. The New Zealand press gave them a good show and even if the NZPA man said, rather strangely, that it was unspectacular, most critics gave the Lions a chance. New Zealand writers, having suffered defeat in South Africa in 1970 were more ready than usual to acknowledge the possibilities, although none could be sure until a few more matches had been played. Indeed, those of the British Press who had seen much before, were prepared to 'wait and see' at this stage and I confess to being one of them, although I admired the optimism of the Management, team and captain. It was healthy, it was good, it was British!

The Press Gang flew in a service plane to Wanganui from Auckland after the Lions had flown direct by charter aircraft, and were able to see from the air the wonderful motorcade of welcome making its way towards the City of Wanganui. More than five thousand people turned out to welcome the tourists who were conveyed to their hotel in vintage motor cars; a gesture that both amused and pleased the tourists, causing Manager Smith, a veteran of the 1950 Lions tour to say, 'Now the tour is really underway!' The Lions had reached Meads Country, the place where the 1966 side had tried to demolish the Meads family legend and failed. Could the 1971 side succeed?

There was a good training session on Monday morning at Spriggens Park and likeable Jim Wallace, who wrote an excellent book on rugby some years ago, was there to watch it with a gathering of his fellow rugby masters in the town. They were an observant, happy group, and were close to the game. Although too polite to say it, one felt they were not impressed with the Lions work-out. Hiller kicked eleven out of eighteen shots at goal and they must have wondered then whether this remarkable English place kicker was as good as the TV suggested. In the late afternoon, with Terry O'Connor and David Frost, I watched the Combined side training under its experienced coach, John Stewart and captain Colin Meads. The side appeared sharp and well together and Meads looked fit although not really exerting himself, but I saw enough to suggest to me that it would be a really hard and, possibly, an even match.

I said as much to the local press and they quoted me below a picture of the three of us who watched the practice. Again, Jim Wallace and his party of enthusiastic school coaches were there and they watched all the training sessions of both sides and the match with equal enthusiasm. It was school holiday time in the town, which houses several public schools for girls and boys, and during the evening Carwyn James, Jim Wallace and several others discussed rugby, past and present, tactics and especially 'climbing in' at the mauls. I said I felt there was no need for this and many forwards were injured as a result of these rather 'wild' methods, no matter in which country they were employed.

Jim Wallace and his colleagues believed it to be fair but I said I would 'blow up' every time were I a referee to save any player from injury from studs. I like my rugby hard but I like it clean. However, such discussions are interesting and the next day NZBC asked me to talk about the match and Colin Meads in an interview and then, in a much longer interview, to discuss world rugby. Everyone in rugby likes talking about the game and I am no exception!

On Tuesday evening the team visited a Maori girl's boarding school and were entertained by some delightful singing while being taught to 'swing the pois'. Best of the team at this difficult art was John Spencer. The morning of the match dawned fine and clear and soon the Rutland Hotel was awake with the busy and friendly staff assisting popular George Earney and his 'support' masseur 'Doc' Murdoch, to get things ready for the big game. Vivian and myself waited for the 'Iron Major' to arrive and to forecast the future in his quiet amusing way, but we did not meet until we got to the ground and it is always good to see Jack Finlay from Fielding.

The team appeared quietly confident and this was especially true of the big forwards, McBride, Roberts and Davies, who believed this was to be their day. Many New Zealanders had suggested that the two props, Lynch and 'Ian' McLauchlan, would not live with the big combined props, McNichol and Whiting, and there was an admirable tension in the air. The Lions just had to make good for it was their second important 'examination'. The management were cool but inwardly concerned for their 'brood' and, win or lose, they wanted a good match, a happy match, and no nonsense. Yet they were acutely aware that the Combined side were hard and that Colin Meads was eager to prove that he was still top 'dog' at forward.

He was playing before his own supporters who naturally, hero-worshipped him and he had led the side in 1966 to victory over the Lions, the first by t Combined XV over a Lions side in New Zealand. Meads had a lot to lose and in a way he was gambling, for he was not really fit after a succession of injuries, and a display below par would lessen his chances of leading New Zealand in the tests. He made no bold forecasts but revealed a keen interest in the Lions, while the local press wrote much about him, and sports editor John Phillips, who gave an excellent party to the visiting press, supplied a detailed potted biography of the 'Pinetree' in the match programme.

Fourth Match
Versus Combined Wanganui–King Country at Spriggens Park, Wanganui, May 26
Lions won by two goals, three penalties and a try (22) to a penalty and two tries (9).
Weather: Fine. *Ground:* Dry and hard. *Crowd:* 23,000 (record).
Teams:
COMBINED XV: J. Wereta; P. Slykerman, L. Virtue, H. P. Milner, I. Milburn; M. Natusch, M. Weinberg; S. McNichol, T. Spry, G. Whiting, C. E. Meads (capt), W. Symonds, M. Rush, J. Knofflock, C. Jackson.
K. Mariner replaced C. Jackson after 15 minutes.
BRITISH ISLES: R. B. Hiller; D. J. Duckham, A. J. Lewis, S. J. Dawes (capt), J. C. Bevan; C. M. H. Gibson, R. Hopkins; S. Lynch, J. V. Pullin, J. McLauchlan, M. G. Roberts, W. I. McBride, J. F. Slattery, T. M. Davies, M. L. Hipwell.
C. W. W. Rea replaced C. M. H. Gibson in second half.
Referee: Mr J. P. Murphy (North Auckland).

Despite all the doubts expressed, the hardness of the Combined side and its determination to repeat the 1966 victory, it was a day of triumph for the 1971 Lions. Virtually, the match was decided in the first five minutes of play. The Lions collected a spanking try after one minute through John Bevan and this, at once, indicated the superior skill and speed of the Lions backs. Duckham gathered in the loose after a kick failed to find touch on the right wing and set off diagonally across field with a dazzling run. He beat several men and then handed on to the galloping Bevan, who simply shot over the line near the left corner. It was a difficult kick for Hiller, but the accurate 'bossman' was in his most determined mood and following his usual careful preparation, toe rubbing against stockings, deep breathing and snorting, he moved forward, bang, and 'over she went' – a lovely goal and five good points.

Shortly afterwards, although we did not know it at the time, Colin Meads got up from a maul slowly, after being on top of the ball, and rubbed his side. It was learned after the match that he had damaged his ribs, and the injury reports developed into a serial.

This injury was to have some effect upon the game, for it did hamper Meads as he looked but a shadow of his true self, and as we were not aware of the latest injury, we believed it to be a combination of injuries suffered in previous months and old age, for he was 35 a few days later. At this stage he may well have retired but, possibly, as with all great players, it could have been a question of personal pride. So much was expected of him, locally and nationally, that he did not want to leave the field of 'battle' and his team to the tender mercies of the devouring Lions but, had he allowed a fit and young substitute to take the field in his place, it may have proved more helpful as John Stewart said afterwards, and not for immediate publication, 'We were not strong enough at lock.' It was dilemma for Meads and even though we did not know then what his future would be in the game, we felt a retirement at Twickenham would have been fitting.

The Lions increased their lead after 13 minutes when Hopkins short punted to the left corner during a rush and the kick was not cleared. Mervyn Davies charged it down and regathered to fall over the line for a corner try which presented another difficult angle for Hiller but, once again, he made no mistake with a beautiful kick bisecting the posts and putting the Lions ten points ahead.

Then the Combined side scored when, during Lions' passing, Dawes missed out Lewis, and Hiller, coming into the line, just could not hold the pass. Milburn on the left wing gathered and raced quite seventy yards for a well deserved try that Rush could not convert. Immediately afterwards, Hiller landed his first penalty goal from 38 yards and a second one from 30 yards and a wide angle after 39 minutes. Rush then kicked a penalty with his second attempt for the Combined side and the interval score was sixteen points to six in favour of the Lions. It was most pleasing for the tourists and well deserved, suggesting quite clearly that the Lions were coming good especially at forward. Their scrummaging was well-controlled and strong, while they charged into the rucks and bound tightly to achieve results.

At this stage we knew the match would be won for there was enough power being generated at forward plus shrewd skill to ensure a good supply of the ball. The backs, if not always smooth in their approach, were too fast and clever for their opponents who did not reveal the speed and confidence of the practice ground. The Lions gathered momentum and when Hiller put them further ahead with his third penalty from 24 yards and straight, after one minute of the second half, it became more of a technical exercise.

Hopkins did splendid work in defence, especially in his own '25', and in probing down the touch-line. Mervyn Davies was in supreme command at the end of the line-out. Duckham and Bevan threatened trouble for their opponents whenever in possession and Hiller dealt more than adequately with the cloud-touching 'up-and-unders' by claiming safe marks and finding good touches out of his own '25'. Unfortunately, after 15 minutes of the second half Gibson was injured in a tackle when he received a knock on the head causing double vision. He was forced to leave the field and his place was taken by Chris Rea.

It took the Scottish player a little time to warm up but he executed several clever probing punts back into the box for Bevan to run on to, and also supported his forwards. The Lions had planned to make it a forward game to prove their ability at matching rugged New Zealand packs – a very necessary exercise! However, as the play developed one felt they could have run the ball more without any danger.

After 34 minutes of the second half Hopkins received from a maul and kicked on cleverly. As the ball came down Rea was underneath it to tap it back to Dawes who ran on and timed a perfect pass, one of the best of the tour, to Bevan who in the words of Doug Smith, 'motored' along at high speed, to score half way out on the left. This time Hiller failed with the kick as he had done with a penalty attempt, to spoil his hundred per cent record for the tour. Before the end, in the sixth minute of injury time Virtue scored a good try for the Combined side that Rush could not convert.

The final score was 22–9 to the Lions and the crowd invaded the field as the teams left it for the dressing room where Meads was examined. At this stage it was suggested that he had sustained broken ribs. He accordingly set off for the local hospital with David Duckham – Meads for an X-ray examination and Duckham, who had played extremely well, for stitches to be put into a cut behind his ear. The Press Gang typed away their messages for the world and there was no small feeling of pride and pleasure among the British Press that the Lions had done so well especially at forward.

John Stewart, the Combined XV coach, was sportsman enough to come to the press seats and praise the Lions. This impressed me and I liked his comment: 'The only way to hold these fellows is to put a bomb in the ball!' The folk at Wanganui are honest, if nothing else, and while Meads was disappointed and in some pain, he did not reveal it when making perhaps his longest, and indeed one of his best, public speeches at the official reception after the match. He praised the Lions and said they would not be beaten easily. He said they were now doing well at forward and studying New Zealand methods, and that it would not be easy for New Zealand in the tests.

There were 'quiet' celebrations at the Rutland Hotel that night, with more noise being made by the Combined team supporters than one would hear at the North British, the Angel and the Shelbourne combined; at least that was the amusing opinion of Manager Smith when we met him the next morning! The Lions had a party in their team room but (South Africa and T.P. please note) there were no broken glasses! However, the next morning there was rumour and counter rumour as to the extent of the injury to Meads, Manager Smith commenting that it was brave to stay on the field, as the player must have been in some pain, but 'foolhardy' because further injury could have proved extremely dangerous. Most of the press sent 'ribs broken' reports but in the end the injury was finalised as torn rib cartilages. What ever it was, it must have been painful.

We spent a quiet day at Wanganui, working, writing letters, and meeting people because we could not leave for Hamilton until late in the evening as there were no planes available. As the

First Taste of the North Island

'Friendships' were too small to take the whole party, the press flew separately, except on the international flights, from the team. This did not worry us unduly but some flights were late, as was this one, and the delay prevented me talking to the Waikato Referees' Association, a fact I much regretted. The chairman of the group was an old friend of mine, Roy Gillies, who had charge of the Second and Third Tests in 1959, plus the memorable North Auckland match, and he was a fair, accurate and popular official.

However, he met us and transported Tudor and myself to the hotel where, until the early hours of the morning, the press were engaged in chatter and song. Tudor, with *Some Enchanted Evening*, earned an encore, Terry McLean rendered a cockney song in a manner that would have pleased Bob Hiller, while cheerful Gabe David was again the MC. Tudor made a great hit with the barmen and they remained on duty for an extra half hour as the Commercial Hotel at Hamilton proved to be another friendly one.

There were letters from home – these are the most welcome feature of a long tour – but several players were still 'waiting'. Mrs Delme Thomas was the most frequent letter writer and Delme rarely failed to arrive at a place without a letter from his family awaiting him. His wife wrote in advance to each hotel and this was the best way. Most players had their letters addressed to the NZRU at Wellington and as they had to be re-routed, it took longer for them to reach the players. I found that second class airmail from the UK took a long time to catch up with me and I missed having the cuttings regularly, although it would be wrong of me to criticise the postal services in New Zealand following the strike and recent decline in Britain; it is sad to reflect, however, that inland services in most countries now falls well below that of the later Victorian Era. Man can get to the Moon in such a short time but it takes longer to deliver letters now than one hundred years ago!

There was a good team training session on Friday morning at Hamilton and a reception for the travelling press from the Waikato Union that was much enjoyed. The ground at Rugby Park was hard and the sun shone strongly while several hundreds of enthusiasts watched the training. One sensed that they had been awakened to the fact that the Lions were no ordinary side. One of the watchers was an old friend, one of New Zealand's deepest thinkers on the game in the 1950's and an outstanding coach, Dick Everest. It was good to talk to him for he was the man who guided Waikato to their Ranfurly Shield victories and also to the memorable win in the first match of the 1956 Springboks tour, which virtually decided the test series.

In that match Dick Everest planned for the first kick to form the first ruck, so allowing Ponty Reid to go away and make the first try, against the Springbok tourists, in New Zealand. I believe they never really recovered from this and, of course, Don Clarke did the rest. Everest talked with me for some time about trends and patterns and it was pleasant to be on the same wavelength. He believes, as I do, that patterns, even successful ones, keep changing. New Zealand, having broken up their tight play for the fifteen man running game, could not tighten it again in South Africa and, perhaps, the change of players rather than approach, was the failure there. Tom Pearce also believed this to be true.

In contrast the Lions, prior to the tour, had prepared methods of tightening their play at forward which had, in the past, always been too loose in New Zealand. Really low, well-bound scrummaging, and forceful driving behind the ball and man at the rucks, was a new feature of these 1971 Lions and Everest was quick to spot this as a change in approach. He wondered, at the time, whether the All Blacks could revert to their earlier methods. The discussion was pleasant and interesting and I admitted to telling Dick Everest that the sight of the Lions doing well at forward, gave me immense pleasure. After preaching the rugby 'gospel' for many years, immodestly perhaps, I was delighted!

Saturday dawned sunny and clear and among the local friends was Howard 'The Friar' Tuck, a farmer from Rotorua who first became a Lions' camp follower in 1959, relatives of Tudor, and Vivian's sister and her family. Ron Hemi and Ian Clarke of the 1963 All Blacks side were at the ground with 26,000 other spectators, which warmed the heart of the local union treasurer. One member said, 'Such a crowd brings back memories of our great days, but we'll give you a game today!'

Fifth Match
Versus Waikato at Rugby Park, Hamilton, May 29.
Lions won by four goals, one penalty, one dropped goal and

Lions *v.* Wellington. Willie John McBride falls to save before a concerted Wellington rush, as Gareth Edwards (9) comes in to cover

The man who set up his backs for a scoring spree against Wellington. Scrum-half Gareth Edwards gets the ball despite a tackle, with Fergus Slattery and Mervyn Davies at the ready

ABOVE: 'The Old Firm.' Most travelled of Lions' rugby critics, Vivian Jenkins and Bryn Thomas chat about previous tours as they wait for their plane 'somewhere in New Zealand'. BELOW: Lions *v.* Otago. Gerald Davies charging away, watched by David Duckham and with the Otago players in hot pursuit

three tries (35) to one goal, one dropped goal and two penalties (14).
Weather: Sunny. *Ground:* Hard. *Crowd:* 26,000.
Teams:
WAIKATO: N. A. M. Pickrang; G. R. Skudder, J. D. Warren, B. A. Stephens (capt), C. A. Anderson; R. D. Stewart, D. E. Phillips; K. H. McBeth, G. W. J. Wright, M. J. Gilmer, K. B. Reay, J. J. Gillett, D. R. Weinberg, D. J. Larner, P. G. Anderson.
BRITISH ISLES: R. B. Hiller; J. S. Spencer, S. J. Dawes (capt), C. W. W. Rea, J. C. Bevan; B. John, G. O. Edwards; R. J. McLoughlin, F. A. L. Laidlaw, S. Lynch, W. D. Thomas, W. J. McBride, D. Quinnell, P. J. Dixon, J. F. Slattery.
A. J. Lewis substituted for Rea for the last half hour.
Referee: Mr P. A. McDavitt (Wellington).

The splendid curtain raiser between Matamata College and Church College set the right tempo for the day and suggested there is nothing wrong with New Zealand rugby if teenagers can play so wisely and well, and in such good spirit. The match ended in a 11–11 draw and there were some players on the field who could well challenge for All Blacks places in the near future.

The Lions began as if they were going to score a century before lunch, at least that was what Bob Irvine said on the air afterwards in his summary. In seven minutes they had produced eight points and those of us in the Lions' Camp were getting ready to say 'This is Der Tag!' but Waikato steadied and we had a most interesting and enjoyable match.

After three minutes Barry John checked, turned back inside, and dropped a lovely goal following a well-timed shove that produced a tight head for the Lions. After seven minutes a pass back from a line-out went astray and Peter Dixon was on to the ball quickly. He shook off a tackle and got near to the posts before sending an overhead pass to the supporting Dawes on his left. The Lions' captain collected his second try of the tour and Hiller kicked an easy goal. The Lions had roared and quite frightened poor old 'Mooloo' recovering from his amusing pre-match antics on the touch-line!

Many of the early scrums had produced tight heads for the Lions and John had two more attempts at dropped goal, but they sailed wide, After 17 minutes Pat McDavitt penalised the

Lions for jumping across at a line-out and an excellent Waikato full-back Pickrang landed a good 48 yard goal but soon Dixon was away again with a clever blindside break from a scrum and although tackled, he slipped the ball to Quinnell who dived over for a good back row forward's try. Hiller could not convert and was well wide with a drop at goal from half way, before Waikato came back at the Lions, strongly, and produced a fine try of quality. Moving to the left, Pickrang entered the line and then left wing Skudder went inside to take a pass at speed. He veered away cleverly to end up near the posts for Pickrang to kick the goal.

Now it was 11–8 and three minutes later the usually reliable Pickrang was wide from 20 yards with penalty attempt. This miss proved to be the turning point in the game, for had the goal been placed then it would have been 11–11 with the Lions back on their heels, but they recovered their poise and drive and went further ahead. Edwards made ground with a short punt, and from the ruck he put Spencer away but he was stopped outside the line. From the line-out the ball came back via McBride to McLoughlin who charged through and over in the corner, only for Hiller's fine kick to drop just the wrong side of the cross bar. So it was 14–8 at the interval.

In the second half it was quite a different story. After nine minutes Spencer was held up at the right corner and from the line-out the ball came back to the Lions. Bevan cut between the centres at top speed to take the pass and race over at the posts like a thunderbolt. Hiller kicked an easy goal and then Rea went off with injured groin to be replaced by Lewis before Bevan got a second try by cleverly leaving his man on the outside. Barry John converted this from the touch-line and then produced a lovely try himself, after being put away by Slattery, for Hiller to convert.

The Lions had now scored 29 points but Waikato were roused once more to collect a fine 50 yard dropped goal by Pickrang and then a 26 yard penalty when Bevan barged his opposing wing into touch after he had kicked ahead. However, Bevan came again for his third try which was not converted and, finally, John kicked another penalty to make the score 35–14 at the end.

It had been a splendid match, full of good rugby, with Waikato ready to run even with a limited supply of the ball. The Lions

First Taste of the North Island

had made mistakes but they scored some splendid tries and the heroes were the hard scrummaging forwards led by McLoughlin, and John and Bevan behind. John brought his tally to 35 points in three matches and Bevan had notched a total of six tries.

There was praise for both sides at the after-match reception and Douglas Smith chatted away with me for the BBC from the local studios where later I received splendid help in cutting tapes for a special piece that would indicate how well the Lions had played, despite two periods when they relaxed, one in each half. The forward drive at the scrum which caused the Waikato props to pop their heads up like 'jacks in the box' and the fine, well-bound rucking was most impressive. The artistry and kicking power of Barry John and the strong running of Bevan stood out, but one felt sorry for Hiller, as it was just not his day, despite three conversions. So the caravan moved on to Auckland again on Sunday after happy farewells to Hamilton and Wakikato following a short but enjoyable stay for the Lions.

On Sunday it was pleasant to share a family lunch with Vivian's sister Dora and her family, for such occasions take one's mind off the tour and provide relaxation. At the same time they can cause even a hardened traveller like myself to feel more than a little homesick, as I must confess to enjoying having my Sunday lunch at home with my family. No hotel can supply quite the same atmosphere!

We drove the 80 miles by car from Hamilton to Auckland, mostly in the rain, with Vivian and myself sharing the driving in the Ford Zodiac, with Messrs James, Frost and O'Connor chatting cheerfully in the back. On the journey we passed the scene of a nasty accident that had occurred only 30 minutes previously, in which five cars were involved. Manager Smith and his team were first on the scene, as their official coach was ahead of us, and he rendered first aid to the injured before the police and ambulances arrived.

A monsoon-like storm hit Auckland soon after we arrived and flooded many roads including the main one from Hamilton, to a depth of several feet, and so we were fortunate in beating the flood. Gabe David, who travelled up on Saturday evening, met Gerald Davies before we arrived and looked after him until the official party could greet him. Having been travelling since Friday, Davies was extremely tired but on taking one of Doctor Smith's 'knock-out' pills and retiring to bed, he was up and about on Monday morning ready for a 'jog' round the practice field. He was keen and eager, saying, 'The Lions are getting a good press back home and I want to get down to it after weeks of study and examinations!'

As it was Whitsunday in the UK, I rang my wife and Gareth at midnight on Sunday from Auckland which was one o'clock lunchtime at home, and chatted to them. I then heard for the first time of the sad accident at the Empire Pool in Cardiff and that Glamorgan cricketer Roger Davis had been given the 'kiss of life' on the square after being struck by a ball. The postal service had been slow and I was behind with the 'news of home'.

Auckland is the most populated city in New Zealand and an interesting place, with the Royal International Hotel caring well for the party and, especially, the staff on the sixth floor who looked after the Press Gang. Three trots a day from the hotel to the post office and back was as good as a 'morning gallop' in the eyes of NZ manager, Frank Kilby. It was good to meet Gerry Peters and his brother and to get a tip for the Great Northern Handicap which was to be run on the Saturday. Frank was keen to get to know the name of the horse and 'put a ring round it' but Gerry didn't tell me the 'hot tip' – only collected my ten dollars with a smile, although my mind flashed back to the successful 'hot tips' Gerry had given to Haydn Morgan in 1959, which kept him in pocket money for the tour.

On the Monday a small 'controversy' broke out because Terry McLean published an article by Dr Manahi Paewai, a former Maori half-back who played against the Lions in 1950, in which he suggested that the Maori international matches should be 'phased out'. His article was interesting but, as it was due to appear in the official programme on the Wednesday afternoon, Auckland RU and Maori officials took umbrage at its 'preview' and when a press party was given at the ARU headquarters, Terry McLean was not invited. This was a domestic matter but, personally, I did not think it was bad enough to 'ban' the rugby writer, although I was not aware of what had 'gone before'.

However, the matter was soon forgotten. Dr Paewai's suggestion was refuted by other Maori rugby leaders although I saw much that was right in it. In New Zealand there is total integration and, as they do not field 'pakeha' or all-white XV's against touring teams, why field all-Maori sides? It is apartheid in reverse and as all provinces include the best Maori players when the Lions are met, as does the national XV, there is no need of it. It is perhaps a 'gesture' to the Maoris by the NZRU but there is no chance, I understand, of a Maori touring side visiting Europe. They did once in the 1920's but the NZRU are now very much against it.

However, the controversy certainly stirred up the fighting traditions of the Maoris, and the local papers were full of it with Maori rugby leaders saying they would maintain the high traditions of their race in the game. On Monday evening Win and 'Chook' Henley and Harold and Betty Potter dined with us at the hotel and there was much discussion about the rival merits of NZ and British rugby, after dinner speakers, and tall tales of the RNVR!

Ray Hopkins had to withdraw on the Tuesday as his injured thigh had not responded to treatment in time and Barry John was partnered by Edwards for the fourth time in six matches on tour. The side prepared itself for a hard match and the rain at Auckland promised a greasy surface, that would not make running and handling at speed an easy task. The NZBC asked me to share the radio commentary with Bob Irvine and I was glad of the opportunity of sitting on top of the grandstand at Eden Park. It gave me an excellent view of the ground and before the match I enjoyed the marching of the Auckland Police Pipe Band, looking more Scottish than the Edinburgh Police. The journey out to the ground had been slow but nowhere near as bad as the great traffic jam at Sydney, although the passengers in the car thought it could be! Unfortunately, the 'jam' was considerable after the match as traffic from the ground met that coming out of town.

Sixth Match
Versus the New Zealand Maoris at Eden Park, Auckland, June 2.
Lions won by a goal and six penalties (23) to four penalties (12).
Weather: Cloudy. *Ground:* Damp and greasy. *Crowd:* 47,500.
Teams:
NEW ZEALAND MAORIS: N. A. M. Pickrang; T. W. Mitchell, K. T. Going, H. P. Milner, K. Carrington; M. A. Herewini,

S. M. Going (capt.); H. F. Maniapoto, R. T. Norton, J. W. Joseph, R. T. Lockwood, J. J. Gillett, V. Baker, L. P. Haddon N. Toki.
K. Marriner substituted for V. Baker in first half.
BRITISH ISLES: J. P. R. Williams; A. G. Biggar, C. M. H. Gibson (capt.), J. S. Spencer, J. C. Bevan; B. John, G. O. Edwards; J. McLauchlan, J. V. Pullin, S. Lynch, G. L. Brown, M. G. Roberts, M. L. Hipwell, T. M. Davies, J. Taylor.
W. D. Thomas substituted for S. Lynch in first half.
Referee: Mr D. Millar (Otago).

Let it be said, immediately, before any analysis is attempted; this was a very hard, vigorous game of rugby football, which any British referee would not have allowed. There were too many flying fists and boots and too much 'climbing-in' at the rucks to satisfy me, or anyone else, used to the firmer control of British referees. Yet Mr Miller was not biased in any way – he just allowed the play to be rougher than, in my opinion, it should have been. Although no complaints were made by the management of the Lions, Mr Miller was quietly crossed off their list of test possibles. Sad, but necessary, although Mr Miller was an excellent fellow in every way. He should have kept a stricter control and tighter rein on the play throughout.

The Lions won in the end because they revealed greater control. The Maori fire disturbed them in the first half and for the first time on tour they fell behind when the Maoris got their third penalty after 36 minutes to make the score 9–6. The Lions equalised before the interval and then went on to win comfortably through the accurate kicking of Barry John.

It was a game of penalties although only twenty-six were awarded in the match when it could have been forty-six. The count was 14–12 to the Lions and they had eight attempts at goal for John to succeed with six, while the Maoris had four attempts and four goals through their excellent full-back, Pickrang. In addition the Lions scored a good try through left wing John Bevan chasing after a deftly-placed short diagonal punt to the left corner. The Lions almost scored four other tries and while coach James modestly declared that it was the result of bad finishing, I was more inclined to believe that it was excellent covering and more than a shade of defensive luck favouring the Maoris!

As always, the Lions began well and were two penalty goals

in the lead after 11 minutes, due to the accuracy of ace kicker John and the indiscretions of the Maoris. After 14 minutes came the Lynch incident. The Irishman was pulling at flank forward Baker, by the jersey, and at this Baker swung round to catch Lynch unawares with his forearm, across the mouth. It was a severe blow that caused blood to spurt from Lynch's mouth as a result of a deep cut, and despite his protests he had to be led away to the touch-line while Gibson, as captain for the day, signalled to Manager Smith concerning a replacement. In a few minutes, Delme Thomas was on the field and Mike Roberts had moved up to prop for Delme to pack with Gordon Brown in the second row.

The arrival of Thomas strengthened the line-out power, for there was Roberts at No. 2, Brown and Thomas in the middle, and Mervyn Davies at the end, and it was this power bloc that turned the scales. In addition they held their own in the set scrums, and here John Pullin did well with one five feet nine inch prop and one six feet four and half inch prop. Pullin, an experienced and effective hooker who gets on with the job, did not lose a strike from the moment he was joined by Roberts and it speaks well of the front row, against a strong trio in Maniapoto, Norton and Joseph.

Barry John and Pickrang each kicked three penalties in the first half and at the interval it was 9–9 but the Lions had not played as well as they should have done and were obviously disturbed by the fiery Maoris. They steadied in the second half and five minutes from the restart achieved the decisive score. John made a long weaving run and then broke out to kick to the left corner. The ball moved wide of defenders and Bevan, in full cry, got to it first to score in the corner for John to kick his best goal of the match and make it 14–9. From that moment, the Lions were in charge. John kicked another two penalties followed by one from Pickrang, and it was 12 minutes before the end when John kicked his sixth penalty to make the final tally 23–12.

Towards the end of the match centre Ken Going raced in and 'took' John Spencer without the ball. It was a thoughtless act and although the referee did not see it, Spencer told him, quite frankly, what had happened. When the Maoris were next in possession and attempted a mid-field scissors, Ken Going dropped the ball when he saw Spencer coming at him. This did not delay Spencer's arrival and the 'compliment' was returned. Strangely enough, a player is not appreciated in New Zealand unless he does 'retaliate'. After this Spencer could have been made a blood brother!

There was a reception after the match; the speakers mentioned a 'hard game' but nothing else, the Lions manager and captain being most diplomatic. They said it was just the type of game they needed at that stage of the tour. They even thanked the referee; such diplomacy 'amazed' the New Zealand press because they wanted and expected a 'knock' story. The Lions be-believed that Mr Miller had allowed too much to 'happen' on the field although he was unbiased, and that they could not have him in the tests, because rough and over-vigorous play would take too great a toll of the Lions. It was as simple as that. The British press sent off their cables and described what they had seen. One looked ahead to the Auckland match with some misgiving. Why was it always rather rough at Eden Park?

The British Press cabled home thousands of words criticising rough play and suggesting that the referee should have been sterner in his approach, while most of the correspondents felt that such vigorous play as was seen, could prove a considerable disadvantage to the Lions if it was repeated in other matches. Again, the Lions management were concerned about refereeing and following good reports of Mr Miller, he appeared now to have lost his place in the test list. Some NZ critics, like Gabe David, said Maori vigour was unnecessary while Terry McLean highlighted the tackle by Ken Going upon an unsuspecting Spencer. Strange as it may appear, the Auckland crowd enjoyed all the 'nonsense', as they did the KO punch by Meads on the diminutive Watkins in the Fourth Test of 1966. Perhaps there is something of the approach of the Madrid 'Corrida' crowd among the folk at Eden Park, which is a magnificent rugby ground.

The Thursday morning press conference saw poor Gabe David working hard in an attempt to get the Lions management to say something about the play in the Maoris match but Doug Smith would give no more than, 'It was a hard match that will do a power of good to the Lions at this stage of the tour especially for those members of the side who have never been to New

Zealand before; however, our discipline and control saw us through to a good victory.'

This was the right approach, of course, and the match had 'steeled' the side for the further battles ahead. One could not but help recall Jim Telfer's famous words at Christchurch following the extremely rough Canterbury match in 1966, followed by an even worse Auckland match! The Lions players had been told by Willie John McBride, earlier in the tour, as to what must be expected in New Zealand and it is possible that until the Maoris match the newcomers did not quite believe him since the first three games had been clean and satisfactorily refereed. After the Maoris match the team and especially those who had the stud marks to prove it, could confirm that there was such a thing as 'climbing in' at the rucks which New Zealanders, unfortunately, do not regard as dangerous play!

In the afternoon we set off for Wellington in an NAC 737 and it was quite a change to travel in a big aircraft again, and the first occasion for me to enjoy bread and cheese snacks with coffee. I really enjoy NZ cheddar cheese and hope the EEC does not prevent supplies of this admirable food reaching the UK!

There was a bonny welcome waiting for the Lions at Wellington Airport with Dick Evans, a tremendous enthusiast, and his silver band blowing away merrily the catchy tune 'When the Saints come marching in!' which is the signature tune of Wellington rugby. There was a good crowd, some flags, and several people dressed up in gear that resembled a 'Mardi Gras'. Best of all, there was a magnificent red London double decker bus to convey the Lions to their hotel. Dick Evans achieved a master stroke with this reception while the City's Parade on Saturday morning before the match was the biggest of the tour.

On arrival at the Hotel St George there was a Rugby Union reception and it was good to meet old friends headed by Tom Morrison, Jack Sullivan, Jack Griffiths, the local officials plus New Zealand's oldest surviving international player and the last of the 1905 team, W. J. 'Billy' Wallace. It was good to hear Tom Morrison pay such friendly tribute to this GOM of NZ rugby at 93 years of age, and to recall that only one Welshman, Willie Llewellyn, also 93, remained alive of the gallant and successful 1905 Welsh XV.

Later that evening Vivian and myself discussed neutral referees with Jack Griffiths, at his lovely house overlooking the harbour, but try as we did we could not convert him to the view that 'neutrality' prevented 'controversy'! Friday was cloudy and Frank Laidlaw was forced to withdraw from the side for the Wellington match with strained knee ligaments in the front of his left leg, sustained in training and he was replaced by John Pullin. A specialist's examination suggested three weeks for recovery and this caused the management to think of a replacement, just in case; David Barry of Oxford University was listed but no formal approach made to the Four Home Unions.

Saturday dawned misty but windless and this was something for Wellington in winter. As the capital City it had enjoyed its best summer since 1918 and so the citizens had prepared themselves for a hard, windy winter, but no winds blew during the Lions first visit, not even a gentle zephyr! The only sad news was that Gabe David had been taken off the tour by his paper, the *Evening Post* on grounds of economy. While I appreciate to the full the economics of the newspaper business and always have tried to maintain a balance as sports editor in what my paper should have and what it could afford, this appeared an unwise decision to me.

Yet the paper does funny things, and I should know, I used to write for it until I dared to criticise NZ rugby as a Welshman! Naturally, Gabe David was deeply upset while I realised how lucky I was to work for the Thomson Organisation and the *Western Mail and Echo* in particular.

Seventh Match
Versus Wellington at Athletic Park, Wellington, June 5.
Lions won by seven goals, two penalties and two tries (47) to two penalties and a dropped goal (9).
Ground: Good. *Weather:* Slightly misty. *Crowd:* 45,000.
Teams:
WELLINGTON: R. J. Gregg; B. M. Koopu, G. A. Batty, R. S. Cleland, M. Cull; J. P. Dougan, I. N. Stevens; G. A. Head, P. Barrett, T. K. McDonald, D. M. Waller, A. E. Keown, J. H. W. Kirby, A. R. Leslie, G. C. Williams (capt.).
BRITISH ISLES: J. P. R. Williams; D. J. Duckham, S. J. Dawes (capt.), C. M. H. Gibson, J. C. Bevan; B. John, G. O. Edwards; R. J. McLoughlin, J. V. Pullin, A. B. Carmichael, W. D. Thomas, W. J. McBride, J. Taylor, T. M. Davies, J. F. Slattery.
Referee: Mr W. Adlam (Wanganui).

First Taste of the North Island

This was a remarkable match. One of the most fascinating I have ever watched in which a Lions side has been engaged. One can be carried away by spectacular play and perhaps over-praise it, but on the Sunday after this match I was still pinching myself to see if I had not been the victim of a rugby 'dream' in which a Lions side did everything right. For years I had waited to see the Lions dominate in such fashion by playing copy book rugby at forward and brilliant running rugby behind, as well as kicking their goals. Everything they did on the field was of a remarkably high quality, from the first moment when Edwards chip-kicked back over the scrum to set up a scoring chance for young Bevan. This was accepted readily with Bevan racing on to the ball at speed, only to be ruled 'off-side' incorrectly by the referee who, when he turned, naturally, saw Bevan in front of him but the wing had started in an 'on-side' position, as O'Reilly had done, so many times before, in 1959, only to be incorrectly 'blown up'. One can understand referees making mistakes and the time lag is very much like 'aim off' when shooting at aircraft in the last war. Fortunately, this error did not matter as the Lions were on the brink of giving a glorious exhibition of match-winning rugby.

After the match I sent a cable to the *South Wales Echo* and then visited the local offices of the NZBC to do a piece for them and take excerpts from the sound commentary. In this I was greatly helped by David Holden and on returning to my hotel, the well-known Hotel St George directed by Frank and Aileen Drewitt, I sat in my room and typed the following piece to convince myself that I had seen a performance that would have earned a 'first' at Oxbridge!

'The latest Lions could become the greatest of any British touring team, since the first British team proper set off in 1904, following their remarkable display against Wellington, one of the top NZ provinces, before 45,000 spectators at Athletic Park, when they won by seven goals, two penalties and two tries to two penalties and a dropped goal. Their performance has set the tour alight and thus they threaten to become the first British Team to win a test series in New Zealand. In all my travels with Lions teams, I have never seen a more convincing display of attacking rugby than that at Athletic Park and must admit that it even surpassed the other high peak achieved by the 1955 side in South

Africa, when it defeated the Orange Free State at Kroonstadt. It took the 1971 Lions half an hour to get the measure of the Wellington side and then they dominated to crush their opponents with sheer pace, precision and power, and a deftness in handling that was truly brilliant.

'It was magnificent and absorbing to watch and whether or not the Lions win the series the memory of this match will remain in my mind, always, as British rugby at its best and most effective. The Lions management were, naturally, overjoyed at the performance yet bravely attempted to hide their joy, saying there were still difficult days ahead, while local officials and national experts kept showering praise, generously and sportingly, upon a side that had earned it. Even Graham Williams, the Wellington captain, showered praise and in this act, he grew in stature as a sportsman, and Wellington accepted their heaviest defeat in history with grace and dignity.'

I discussed the match with Carwyn James and John Dawes and realised that the Lions now had confidence in themselves and that it was the turn of New Zealand to worry. One man who regained his confidence was Gareth Edwards. He was the key man in this running display, for his long and accurate passes set it up for the backs to run elusively because he put them clear of opposing loose forwards. He had done this all winter for Wales and given Barry John the space, time and freedom he required to reveal his genius. Since he was subduing his own natural genius, many were tempted to forget the important part played by Edwards.

He did a great deal more against Wellington, which caused Jack Finlay to comment 'This Edwards is a good one. What a different player from that of 1969!' The 'Iron Major' never overpraises and the Edwards 'breaks' were interesting and threatening. John of course, was just 'King' John, with all the time in the world to manoeuvre and plan and dart and kick. He made use of the beautiful service to reveal the full array of his talents and ended the match with another 19 points in his locker, bringing it to 74 for the tour in the five matches he had played.

Mike Gibson had his best match, as an attacking Lion, for he made full use of the freedom he enjoyed, the passes given him, and the situations created by forwards and halves, to run delightfully. He scored two tries and converted one and it was a 'new look' Gibson because he never gets the chance to run in International rugby when playing for Ireland. In this match he took his chances readily to flash away while the steady Dawes, thinking all the time and 'reading' the play, revealed how necessary he was for the side as its unobtrusive leader.

The fiery John Bevan on the wing looked a test try-scorer and for a 20-year-old was strong and determined, with magnificent acceleration and swerve. When he turned inside for one of his four tries, he produced a touch of high skill not expected from one so young in the game at top level. The crowd loved to see him running even though his tries spelled heavy defeat for their own side.

John Williams at full-back thoroughly enjoyed himself after half an hour of solid defence, and kept joining the line and bursting through. He shared in the points spree, with a last minute conversion from the touch-line. David Duckham went 'inside' to make two of the tries but had few passes himself as the play did not move to the right very often. By habit the ball generally moves to the left when right-handed players are in action, and this was true of Newport when Roy Burnett was at his best, for it was John Lane on the left wing who got all the tries, rather than Ken Jones on the right!

The Lions forwards were in splendid form with Ray McLoughlin and Willie John McBride controlling affairs and all eight played well, individually, and as a unit, to run the Wellington pack off their feet. When it was all over I felt that this was the first peak in the graph of form and that it could be reached again, perhaps, on two other occasions, and one hoped that it would be the First and Third tests. However brilliant the display, and however keen the side was to repeat it, there are so few days in rugby football when all fifteen players in a side are inspired to give of their best. This day was really one of them and I was grateful for the pleasure it gave to me. It was a reward for years of touring 'in the darkness'.

The Lions led Wellington at half-time by eighteen points to three and won in the end by 47 points to nine. For the record the scorers in the match were – for the Lions – Bevan (4), Gibson (2), Taylor, John, Carmichael, tries; John five conversions, two penalties; Gibson and Williams one conversion. For Wellington –

Gregg, a brave full-back, two penalties and Dougan, a steady first five eighth, one dropped goal.

Thus ended the first visit to the North Island but the South Island or 'mainland' appeared reluctant to welcome the Lions and shrouded its vast stretches of green grass with fog!

CHAPTER FIVE

Into the Deep South

New Zealanders who live there call the picturesque South Island the 'mainland', and they look upon the North as the offshore Island, which causes a great deal of banter between the two groups. However, many born in the South Island are now living in the North, and there is a gradual migration of young people northwards. Yet the South Island is so much like Scotland that one would think one was much nearer home, than 13,000 miles away, when one hears the gentle burr of true Scottish accent in Invercargill, the southernmost city in the Commonwealth.

Yet on Sunday June 6, the South Island appeared more than reluctant to accept the 1971 Lions because shrouds of thick fog closed down the airports at Christchurch and Timaru, and even Dunedin further south, but not Invercargill. Wellington R.U. liaison officers informed Manager Smith of the situation and he replied, 'Unless we can fly straight into Timaru, we'll wait until tomorrow. I do not want to be travelling all over the country and have my team too tired to play.' In this he was right because the match had been arranged for Monday instead of Wednesday and he could not take any chances.

John L. Sullivan, chairman of the N.Z.R.U. Council, came into see Manager Smith after he and 22 players had returned from Wellington Airport, and it was agreed, without any bother, to fly out on Monday via Christchurch and play on Wednesday. Many folk had travelled to Timaru to give the Lions a special South Island Sunday welcome, including Jack Manchester, but they returned home and the local team was dispersed to meet again on Tuesday. The Lions duly flew to Christchurch on the Monday by charter plane and trained there before travelling on by coach to Timaru. The Press Gang split up into three groups and drove straight to Timaru and there enjoyed the friendliness of the Hydro Grand Hotel and the local hospitality provided by Bert Rippin and Jack Strang.

When the Lions arrived the management held a press conference at the hotel and Carwyn James pointed out that all the party were aware of the danger of becoming complacent, as a result of the big win over Wellington and suggested that what was needed, to prepare the Lions for the test atmosphere, was some harder matches at forward and he admitted quite humbly, 'We cannot afford to think that we can beat the All Blacks forwards, easily. There is still much to be done to improve our forward play and we are well aware of it.'

A New Zealand press man suggested that New Zealand would change their tactics for the test series and play a much tighter game, and to this Coach James replied that he was not concerned at any possible tactical change by the All Blacks but to get the Lions forwards to their peak by the first test. He was aware of the lessons of the 1965 tour when the Springbok backs were good but the forwards not quite good enough to hold the All Blacks. Again, the All Blacks won all their matches in 1970, outside the tests, but failed in the test series because they were not good enough.

The Lions had no room for complacency at this stage for it needed a very special effort at forward to survive in the test series and James set his mind towards this end. Chatting to him, privately, I found him well aware of each player's strength and weakness on the field, and personality off it. He was eager to keep everyone happy and to share to the full the life of the party, but he knew some players were better than others and, at this stage, the choice of the test team could be limited to twenty members even though all but one of the party were internationals. More than anything else, he was aware of the danger of possible injury to half a dozen key players, which would disturb the whole side and rob of them of the chance of test success. Injury to his 'protegé' Barry John, would be near-disaster! James presented a cool front; a nonchalant one almost, when talking rugby but, inside, he was concerned, deeply, and as a Welshman, emotionally, but experience had taught him 'to play it cool.'

Frank Laidlaw, who had injured himself in training before leaving Auckland during the previous week had flown direct to Invercargill and then back by coach to Dunedin for special treatment for strained ligaments in the front of his knee. At first there was concern for his possible absence for some weeks and the

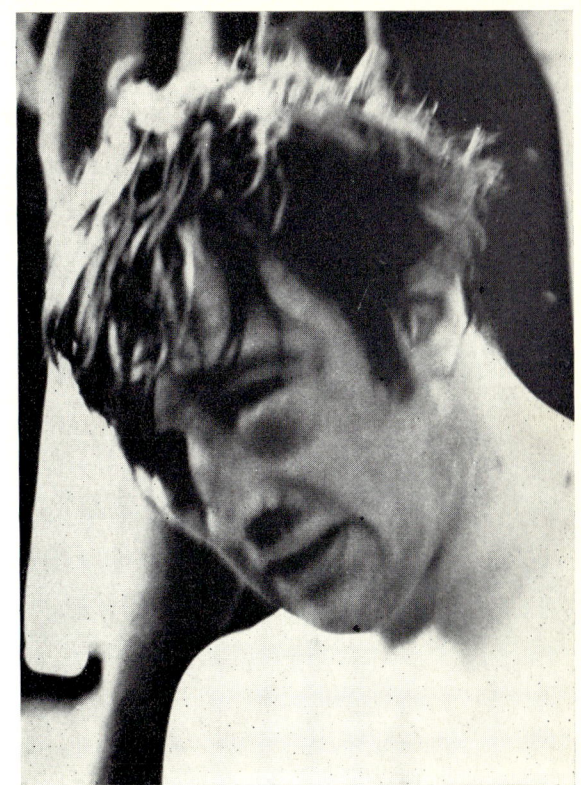

The price of victory. Sandy Carmichael, the Lions' prop, with blackened eyes after the Canterbury match. Photograph taken by John Taylor in the dressing rooms immediately after the match

BELOW: David Duckham dives over for one of his six tries *v.* West Coast/Buller at Greymouth, a scoring feat which created a new Lions' record

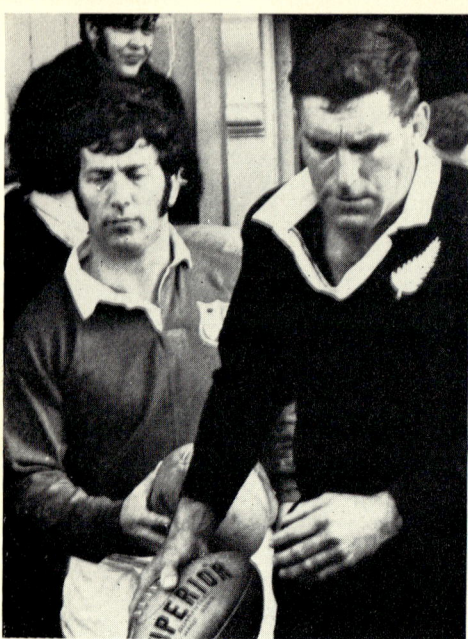

The First Test. Rival captains, John Dawes and Colin Meads, lead their sides out on to Carisbrooke Park, Dunedin, for a memorable match

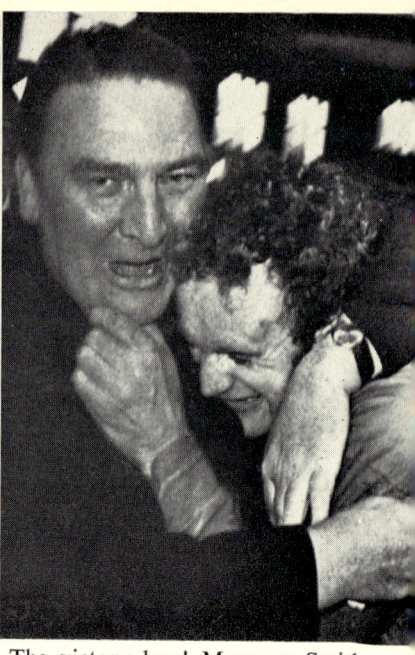

The victory hug! Manager Smith, overwhelmed with emotion at victory in First Test, hugs centre Mike Gibson, as did all players in turn, as they entered dressing room after the match

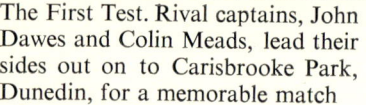

The brave replacement. Ray Hopkins, who took over, after ten minutes, for the injured Edwards at scrum-half in the First Test, sends out a pass to Barry John from a line-out. The Lions' forwards are Davies, Dixon and Thomas

necessity for a replacement, but when the party eventually arrived at Dunedin on Thursday he was prepared to 'jog only' and this cheered the management, for John Pullin and Frank Laidlaw were particularly important men in the forward set up, as two experienced, fair striking hookers.

Timaru is a friendly place and in summer a lovely holiday resort. Tudor James and I inspected the beach and the docks, and with Vivian were entertained by Harold Coxhead and his family together with former All Black Gordon Lawson and *Timaru Herald* proprietor, Edward Kerr. Indeed, a long evening started with the largest whisky I have ever had in my life. The tumbler must have contained five 'doubles' and, as Harold Coxhead remarked, 'It gets right down to your navel!' Later in the evening back at the hotel, I realised how right he was and moved quietly away to my bed but not before Tudor 'blindside' James had moved away before me! Such are the hazards of touring in a friendly land!

Wednesday dawned a little misty but with promise of fine weather, and by the time the match was due to start it was beautifully sunny in the true manner of the South Island. There was a winter crispness in the air and it was easy to realise why New Zealand is such a healthy place to live in. The air is so pure; no smog, but even New Zealand, which must have pleased the Duke of Edinburgh on his several visits, is starting to complain of pollution. This is sad, for there can be no land populated by British people that is so near to 'God's little acre', and whatever be the future of the land, it must survive as it is, for nowhere else in the world can there be such a healthy yet simple standard of living.

Eighth Match
Versus Combined South Canterbury, Mid Canterbury, North Otago at Fraser Park, Timaru, June 9.
Lions won by two goals, two penalties, three tries (25) to two tries (6).
Weather: Sunny. *Ground:* Firm. *Crowd:* 13,000.
Teams:
COMBINED XV: N. Twaddell; J. Greenslade, P. Gard, P. Roddick, B. Carlyon; A. O'Neill, A. Soloman; J. Wilson, K. Milne, G. Predergast, M. Hanham, D. Grant, T. Lister (capt.), R. Noble, A. Stuck.

BRITISH ISLES: R. B. Hiller; T. G. R. Davies, J. S. Spencer, A. G. Biggar, D. J. Duckham; C. W. W. Rea, R. Hopkins; J. McLauchlan, J. V. Pullin, A. B. Carmichael, G. L. Brown, M. G. Roberts, D. L. Quinnell, P. J. Dixon, M. L. Hipwell.
Referee: Mr J. R. Innes (Counties).

Invariably, on tour, it is extremely difficult for a side to play well following upon a major triumph such as the Lions produced at Wellington. In fact it is extremely difficult to do so, and on many tours it has been the case of 'after the Lord Mayor's show....' Although the Lions won this match comfortably enough, at 25–6, which looks good in the records, they did not play anywhere near as well as they should have done. They could have won by forty points to six but instead the backs, and especially the halves, kicked far too frequently, and as a result of this, two fine try-scoring wings, Duckham and Davies, received very few chances.

One expected a hard match from the Combined side as in the three previous tours, and their forwards played well. Yet the Lions pack got enough good ball which was wasted, unfortunately, by kicking, and often kicking that went straight into the arms if full-back, Twaddell. One does not seek to be over critical of Chris Rea who was back in the side after a break through injury, and playing away from his normal position which was centre. His full confidence had not returned and one feels that Spencer as captain for the day should have demanded passing, rather than kicking.

Lions should have won this match by many more points because players had ability to have done so but just lacked application in the particular circumstances. Often lesser sides on tour can be beaten by continued handling and running, and switching of attacks from left to right and back again, and varying the nature of point of attack and switch. No instructions had been given for kicking and in any case there should have been a little more purpose in the kicking, with the ball either placed away from the full-back for the wings to run on to, or higher, so that the forwards could get under it.

Combined side had some useful players, for Soloman at scrumhalf and O'Neill at first five knew what it was about, while Gard was a good strong centre. Had the wings greater pace they might have scored a few tries but as it was the Lions cover defence was too quick for them, even though Hiller was caught, occasionally, out of position. As always at Timaru, the Combined forwards worked hard and Referee Innes did not miss a great deal, so that the battle at forward was keen but clean. The 'mighty mouse' as Manager Smith christened Ian (John) McLauchlan, did a notable job as prop and Gordon Brown won plenty of good ball at the line-out, while the back row marauded well enough even though Quinnell was not quite one hundred per cent fit.

No real blame could therefore be attached to the forwards, and it was at half-back that Lions made things hard for themselves. Hopkins scored an excellent try after a 35 yard run from the open side of the scrum and also made several other elusive runs. However, his service, if quick, was not of a particularly great length and Rea may have felt he was harnessed by standing up close. However, Hopkins and Rea over-kicked when a swift flowing service to the wings, which was the team talk intention, would have succeeded.

Again, Hiller often came into the line because he played a rather 'roving' game at full-back, as if he wanted to be continually in the play! One admired his initiative but, occasionally, things became confused and, often, when entering the line he had to wait for Duckham to come up for the pass and this slowed things down considerably.

Gerald Davies, in his first match of the tour on the right-wing, had only two chances and he took them readily to collect two fine tries. Duckham got one really good try through foraging and then showing his true speed. New Zealand press were strong in their criticisms and, even if it was a 'lacklustre' performance as David Phillips would say, it was not quite fair to judge it against the Wellington match which was quite remarkable and not easily repeated. John Brooks of the *Christchurch Press* said, 'Ragged Lions XV play uninspiring football'. Dudley Manning in *Otago Daily Times* said, 'Lions Timaru Performance lacked Expected Sparkle,' and the *Timaru Herald* man – who appeared to be just a shade biased – said, 'The British Lions survived rather than overcame its first South Island opposition' ... but it was not really like that. The Lions should have collected forty points!

At the after-match reception, John Dawes said it was the hardest match of the tour up to that time, at least in New Zealand, and in this he was right while Manager Smith commented, 'The match was an anti-climax after Saturday but it was a win, and 25 points to six will look good in the record book.' Tom Lister, the All Black and Combined captain said, 'The scrummaging and rucking of the Lions was a lesson for us but I feel we gave away a few points.'

In the first half Ray Hopkins, David Duckham and Gerald Davies scored tries and Hiller converted two and kicked a penalty against a penalty by Twaddell for the Combined side. In the second half Hiller kicked a penalty for the Lions and Gerald Davies and Chris Rea scored tries, while Twaddell kicked another penalty for the Combined.

Thirteen thousand spectators watched the match and appeared to enjoy it in good conditions, with the sun shining strongly into the stand and making it rather difficult for the Press to observe many of the finer points. The healthy partisanship of the crowd and the drinking that went on afterwards at the various bars in the town suggested that rugby habits are the same in most parts of the world, from Llanelli to Invercargill, from Vancouver to Sydney and Murrayfield to Newlands!

After a press conference at Timaru early on Thursday morning we set off in the rental car, a larger one this time, driven by Vivian and we reached Dunedin safely after a 'comfort' stop at Omahru, to make our headquarters at the Southern Cross Hotel, a most comfortable hostelry, run with a smile by manager Bill Percival. The hotel is most comfortable and the staff both charming and efficient.

Our many good friends in Dunedin include Jack and May Manchester, Charles Saxton, Vic Cavanagh, Willis Perriam Arthur Marslin and his wife from Alexandra, and many others. It is a real rugby city; the home of rucking and the modern forward game as played in New Zealand and, of course, Carisbrooke Park where I had never seen a British side succeed. Yet I like the place, even though the Lions lost there in 1959 by 18–17! One holds no grudges now, although much has been written in hard criticism of that day in 1959. New Zealand has accepted it as a 'black day', and even Jack and Victor feel it should be forgotten.

On Friday it was a day of rumour and counter rumour, as first

Ray McLoughlin pulled out with renewed leg trouble and then Mike Gibson with groin trouble, while even Barry John was doubtful at one time. The shadow of defeat loomed before us again to threaten the pleasure of our visit. Next came a 'will he, won't he' query concerning Keith Murdoch, the Otago All Black prop, who had played in his test in South Africa in 1970 suffering from appendicitis! He did, in fact, withdraw on the Saturday morning from the Otago team. Obviously, his power would be missed in the front row, while the heavy showers of rain threatened a wet surface at the Park and a heavy ground which, despite all beliefs, was of little or no advantage to the Lions, who preferred a dry ground.

On Friday afternoon, Carwyn James and Vic Cavanagh had a two hour discussion at Vic's office, and I was delighted at this for Ray Williams had spent much time with Vic in 1970 and Vivian and I had spent many hours over the years discussing rugby with him, but alas, the 1966 Lions did not put themselves out to talk with him, when he could and would have done so much to help. In 1959 Vic and Jack convinced Vivian and myself of the value of true rucking, and we preached the gospel in Britain but officials and players paid only temporary attention to it. Not until Ray Williams, who did so much for the Rugby Union and the coaching manual from 1964 onwards, came as coach organiser to the W.R.U., was the message from New Zealand understood and put into practice. I feel now that British Rugby will never fall so far behind again.

In any case Saturday June 12, was going to produce the real challenge, for Otago, the top ruckers in New Zealand as a provincial side, were keen again to achieve a victory, that would be their fourth successive one against the Lions. Their admirable coach, Arthur Watson, followed along the lines of the Cavanagh family and Charles Saxton. He knew his job and had laid it on... 'Tackle hard, get to the breakdown quickly and, as a whole pack, ruck the ball quickly!' This was the established Otago pattern and all New Zealand waited to see how it would go and whether the Lions, after all their early success, could counter and hold Otago, a side so effective at the basic methods of New Zealand forward play.

Otago did not worry about the rain and the heavy ground, or even the loss of Murdoch, but at dinner on Friday, Jack Manchester appeared more than concerned when he said, 'I believe your forwards know much more about it. They are better organised and your inside-backs are good. You may give us a bit of the "hurry up" but it should be a fine game. I rather fancy your chaps!' This was not good old-fashioned New Zealand 'propaganda' to get favourable odds for a friendly bet, but an honest assessment and to some extent it encouraged Vivian and myself, but we still had a nagging doubt deep down, for Carisbrooke Park appeared to hold a bogey for Lions' sides.

Ninth Match
Versus Otago at Carisbrooke Park, Dunedin, June 12, 1971.
Lions won by three goals, a dropped goal and a penalty (21) to a penalty, a dropped goal and a try (9).
Weather: Sunny. *Ground:* Heavy and drying. *Crowd:* 29,000.
Teams:
OTAGO: L. W. Mains; B. A. Hunter, G. Sims, D. J. Robertson, M. P. Collins; A. J. Clark, G. L. Colling (capt.); L. A. Clark, D. A. Pescini, J. D. Mathieson, W. W. Townsend, M. A. Atkinson, R. Smith, G. W. McGee, J. C. Adams.
D. A. Lingard and P. Docherty substituted for D. A. Pescini and Mathieson in the second half.
BRITISH ISLES: J. P. R. Williams; T. G. R. Davies, S. J. Dawes (capt.), D. J. Duckham, J. C. Bevan; B. John, G. O. Edwards; J. McLauchlan, J. V. Pullin, A. B. Carmichael, G. L. Brown, W. J. McBride, M. L. Hipwell, P. J. Dixon, J. Taylor.
Referee: Mr J. G. Pring (Auckland).

An air of excitement prevailed from first whistle to last in this splendid match, won in the end, and deservedly so, by the Lions, but not before a lighter Otago side had put up a magnificent fight. It was, at this stage, easily the hardest match of the tour but remarkably clean for one of such intensity. Otago had made good their coach's promise that they would run with the ball and this they did most effectively.

All thirty-two players (Otago had to have two substitutes through injury) knew they had been in a real rugby match and the crowd enjoyed every moment of it. Referee Pring entered into the spirit of the occasion and when, at the end, Jack Manchester said he had not enjoyed a match more for ten years, I believed him. Perhaps, my views were coloured by the fact that I had witnessed a victory for a Lions side at the ground for the first time, but I was proud of British rugby after this one. Victory had been won at the home of rucking, and this merely added to the pleasure I had experienced at Wellington!

Manager Smith and Coach James were delighted with the success, and Doug Smith told me before I said a few words on N.Z.B.C. T.V. at the ground, 'It's wonderful, Bryn!' and that moment we were kindred souls, as we shook hands, for it had been a long wait for both of us who had watched matches at the ground before and seen the Lions lose. Yet Otago had shown the same magnificent spirit as in previous matches, only this time the Lions had been taught and coached, and imbued with the right spirit, not only to survive, but to conquer.

The pack stuck to its guns superbly and never faltered even though the lighter Otago eight were quicker over the rather heavy, holding turf. Without Ray McLoughlin, Delme Thomas and Mervyn Davies, who had played there before, this was a fine achievement. McBride had a great day and was, possibly, the best all-round forward on the field. Taylor led well and was lively, while Brown, Pullin and Dixon shone. Yes, all eight worked hard that day and although Hipwell said to me afterwards in his lovely Irish brogue, 'That was a hard one... I could do with a good sleep now... I have many bruises!' the Lions had stood up to it, physically, remarkably well and the 'Mighty Mouse' John (Ian) McLauchlan did not suffer because of his lack of inches.

The front row held its own and it was two of the Otago men who had to retire with injuries, hooker Pescini and prop Mathieson, although these were not the result of foul play, However, all eight Otago forwards, or perhaps I should say ten, charged into the rucks and after the loose ball like a swarm of bees. They never eased up and won enough good ball for their backs to hammer away at the Lions defence for long periods. They often got close to the Lions' line and won the ruck there, only to be held up by the stout-hearted tackling of all, but especially that of John Williams who produced his usual fearless game. Many New Zealand pressmen made the ruck 'count' 14–5 to Otago but this was way out. It may have been 12–10 and some made it 12-all, but their counting caused them to over emphasise Otago's ability in the rucks, for as Victor Cavanagh told me afterwards, 'The Lions forwards have learned to ruck!'

No longer were the Lions pushed back in the rucks, as on previous tours. They stood their ground and forced Otago to rake the ball, or win it themselves, and this was the greatest progress that had been made. Again, they bound at the rucks and stopped entering them at the sides, but got round behind and gave the ruck their weight. Actually, rucking New Zealand style is a simple thing and particularly uncomplicated, but it needs a pack to get to the tackle or breakdown in sufficient numbers to make it effective.

One would agree that Otago were slightly faster over the ground but the Lions halves had a great day. Edwards was immensely strong at the base of the scrum and had a worthy opponent in Lindsay Colling, but his long pass, his short bursts, his clever kicks, and one long diagonal open-side break round the end of the line-out to make a try for Dawes, was vintage Gareth! This was the match that re-established him in New Zealand, and Jack Manchester could now acknowledge why a 'one-eyed Welshmen had given him such praise in Europe... he's a good boy... I like him... that long pass... makes it difficult to get at John... and he's a beaut!'

Barry John, was just... 'King John'... playing easily and shrewdly and having more time to do things than anyone else, even when under pressure. How the crowd yelled when he was caught, on only just a few occasions, but Otago could not keep his magical right boot quiet and he was banging away merrily at goal throughout the match to collect valuable points. He added twelve to his tally to become the highest scoring Lion in New Zealand, after only five matches, passing Malcom Thomas's previous record of 73 in 1950.

Behind them the three-quarter line took its chances and tackled well even though the try-scoring Welshmen, Bevan and Davies, on the wings did not collect any tries. Dawes and Duckham tackled manfully while Williams crashed his men to earth and never faltered when catching the high ball. It was a good performance, even though the Lions had been thoroughly tested to reveal items in their play which could be improved upon since the opposition would be harder still in the tests.

John put the Lions ahead after five minutes with a forty yard penalty goal before Otago replied with an excellent try by left-wing Collins. The Lions did not take the lead again until after 25 minutes, and then came a splendid combined movement, ending with Taylor scoring a try and John kicking a good goal. Next came a good left-footed dropped goal from Mains before John dropped a thirty yard goal after quick possession had been gained from a line-out, and it was 11–6 at the interval.

The vital score for the Lions came after seven minutes of the second half, when Pescini was off the field and had not been substituted. They forced play down near to the right corner where the Lions won a tight head scrum and Edwards shot to the blindside and put John Williams, who came into the movement, crashing over. Better still, John converted this from near the touch line, a lovely kick, right through the middle and the Lions were 16–6... and it needed two scores for Otago to get on terms again.

Edwards was penalised for picking the ball out of a scrum and Mains kicked a good angled goal from the '25' line to make it 16–9, only for the Lions to make the match safe, ten minutes later. Edwards set off round the end of a line-out and handed-off tackler after tackler, as he ran diagonally, Dawes stayed with him and took the final pass just outside the line to dive over for a try that John had no difficulty in converting.

We had twenty minutes more of play that was always exciting, and although Mains failed with a couple of penalties as the Otago forwards got near to the line, they could not reduce the leeway, try as they did. Eventually, the final whistle went and it was a group of very tired players that left the field. As soon as the reception was over, Carwyn James and John Dawes joined me at the N.Z.B.C. studios and they talked to London and to Cardiff, and Peter Sellers was there, Dunedin's sports memory man and radio organiser, to enjoy it all. It was a happy day and there was a musical atmosphere at the team's dinner that night!

It was early in the morning when we left Dunedin for Greymouth on Sunday, far too early for me, as I do not enjoy jumping out of bed at 6 a.m. Although I did not normally take breakfast on tour, this was one of the mornings when a 'Continental' was necessary! We flew to Christchurch, where it was raining and most dismal, and had to wait a few hours for the Hokatika plane to take us across the Plain and over the Alps into the West Coast, which is completely different from the rest of New Zealand.

D

It is a mining area created by the Gold Rush of 1865 and for a Welshman it was easy to accept the coal trucks being shunted to and fro in front of the hotel, the craggy faces of men who had spent most of their lives searching for minerals, and the friendly atmosphere and detachment from the way of life in other parts.

We stayed at the hotel of Ron King the former, powerful All Black lock, who played between 1934 and 1938 and was in Manchester's team that lost to Wales in the memorable match of 1935. His son, Jeffrey, cares for the hotel now, and Ron spends a great deal of time with his flowers, potted plants and gold panning. He has a 'claim' and he works it with an 'offsider', Johnson, and as he said, 'Gold is still attractive to man, and he will always seek it. It has a fascination and we get hundreds of visitors to the West Coast, who want to hear all about the Gold Rush days of over one hundred years ago. We run our claim as a hobby but the history of it all is most interesting.'

The ground was heavy for team training on Monday and during the evening I spoke to the Hokatika Rotary Club and enjoyed their company. Tuesday saw the team visit the Franz Joseph Glacier, one of the great sights of New Zealand. Those members who did not travel played golf and, despite sharp showers of monsoon quality, Vivian and Tudor joined a competition run by Booth's Gin company and a good time was enjoyed by all. David Frost and myself walked along the grey sanded beach in the bright sunshine and talked about newspapers and other sports, anything but rugby, and the evening was spent in celebrating 'McLean's Reprieve'. Having been banned by the Auckland R.U. he was 'reprieved' after four days but I do think it was a 'storm in a tea cup' and could have been avoided by the *New Zealand Herald* who, acting out of courtesy, could have requested formal permission to use part, or the whole, of Dr Paewai's article, Simple omissions lead to major outbursts and rugby does not benefit. Maybe New Zealand papers expect too much of their Rugby Unions but one senses that they could be kinder towards one another in Auckland, as I feel sure there are faults on both sides!

The weather was 'inclement' on Tuesday night and early Wednesday morning, and gave Rugby Park at Greymouth a fair soaking but at least the morning was fine, if threatening, and the arrival of Bill Craddock on the scene was enouraging and gave a mayoral touch to proceedings and enabled two N.Z.R.U. council members to 'talk trotts'. Huddled in the corner of the King's Hotel Bar, Craddock and Kilby, 'experts in horse flesh', adopted a conspiratorial air, as they discussed in hushed voices the horses, the riders, the going, and other matters for Saturday's big night at Christchurch. Frank Kilby did not know that Vivian and myself were to win 15 dollars apiece by putting ourselves 'in the hands of the maestro', while Frank could not find Bill for the 'whispered tip' at the Canterbury Park Trotting Club during the winter meeting. Having had no news from Gerry Peters and our ten dollars apiece in Auckland, we celebrated our 'considerable' success on Sunday at Blenheim. It is more fun when you know nothing about the runners or riders, and many Lions backed *David Frost*, for obvious reasons, but he could do no better than get second place!

Tenth Match
Versus Combined West Coast – Buller at Rugby Park, Greymouth, June 16.
Lions won by six goals one penalty and two tries (39) to one penalty, one try (6).
Weather: Cloudy. *Ground:* Heavy with grass. *Crowd:* 4,500.
Teams:
COMBINED XV: G. W. Hart; C. Skates, L. B. Halsall, B. Stewart, R. Alexander; K. J. Beams, M. McQuillan; D. G. Bryce, J. R. Tacon, B. Hearsey, D. Evans, R. Forsyth, D. Stevenson, J. W. Halsall, A. Fussell.
BRITISH ISLES: R. B. Hiller; D. J. Duckham, S. J. Dawes (capt), C. W. W. Rea, A. G. Biggar; A. Lewis, R. Hopkins; J. F. Lynch, J. V. Pullin, J. McLauchlan, W. D. Thomas, M. G. Roberts, P. J. Dixon, D. Quinnell, J. Taylor.
Referee: Mr R. J. Oswald (Bay of Plenty).

John Spencer and Gordon Brown had been forced to withdraw during the morning, for Spencer had a pulled hamstring, and Brown was suffering from sinus and ear trouble. Their places were taken by David Duckham, who was to run into rugby history, and John (Ian) McLauchlan, who never turned in a poor performance and, like Hughie McLeod before him, was an honest toiler with an optimistic approach.

The match became known as 'Duckham's Day' for the long-striding English three-quarter, with his blond hair flowing behind in the slipstream of his moving body, gave a tremendous impression of speed on the rugby field. He collected six tries to create a new record for a Lions player as a try scorer in one match, and also for any visiting player in New Zealand. He fell short by two of the record set by Ron Heeps for New Zealand in a country match in Australia, but had the Lions maintained their first half momentum in the second half, Duckham could have scored a dozen or at least ten! The Lions eased off a little and the Combined side improved. Then, later, the Lions found difficulty in getting back into the game after scoring 31 points in the first half and in the second they could do no better than collect eight, to six by the Combined.

During the first half the Lions forwards won much good possession at the line-out and the backs moved the ball smoothly to Duckham on the right-wing, and his speed did the rest. He collected five tries while Biggar on the left-wing, with fewer chances, scored only one try. Bob Hiller was in superb form as a place kicker; accurate and strong, and the ball sailed high between the post for five consecutive conversions and a penalty, which was a magnificent exhibition of the art. In contrast to many other grounds in New Zealand, the four thousand five hundred spectators at Rugby Park, Greymouth cheered his efforts and were sporting enough to recognise rugby ability.

John Pullin was to have had a rest in this match but owing to the withdrawal of Gordon Brown, he had to play again and it speaks much for his fitness, strength and dedication, in his own special quiet West Country manner, that he was to play six matches in succession as Frank Laidlaw was injured, and these six included those against the Maoris, Wellington, Otago and Canterbury. No Lions team could have got more from a man than they did from honest John Pullin at this stage of the tour, and I feel he was proud to have given such service.

After six minutes of the second half, John Taylor had to leave the field with a pulled hamstring in his right leg, and Fergus Slattery took over. At first one thought that Taylor would be out for some time but he made good progress although the casualty list was extremely long at this stage with nine players affected for one reason or another.

It was an exceptionally clean match and the Combined side played up bravely and enthusiastically during the last twenty minutes. In fact they collected one of the rare tries conceded by the Lions early in the tour, and it brought a resounding cheer from a crowd that was not too partisan. When the final whistle went the West Coast had reason to be pleased with itself, and the local union members were happy because the score had not been as heavy as it was at Wellington! At this stage everyone in the other provinces appeared to be basing their efforts upon those of Wellington, and perhaps this was a little unkind, as the Lions had been world beaters at Athletic Park, and it was not easy for anyone to forget such a memorable display.

Hart kicked a penalty goal for the Combined side early in the second half and Stewart scored the try near the end which Hart could not convert. Duckham scored six tries, Biggar one and Hiller one, for the Lions, while Hiller converted six of them and kicked a penalty goal. Both he and Duckham collected 18 points which was a remarkable achievement and suggested that English rugby was far from dead and that the old country would have need of these two men for many years to come. The Lions were immensely pleased that these two players had done well and especially 'Bossman' Hiller whose ready wit, and self criticism, made him a good tourist and a popular character. Obviously, he was intensely keen to play in a test but never once in two tours did he complain to anyone that he just 'missed out', as New Zealanders say.

Thursday morning saw the first and only appearance of the 'Barber', a wind so sharp and cold that it cuts the skin. The Lions went off to train and take lunch at Hokatika but as the Welsh Press 'mafia', as they called Vivian, Tudor and myself had much work to do, we remained behind to type away, study the papers, write letters, pack bags and talk once again with Ron King about the West Coast and gold mining.

Most of the papers had suggested that the Lions lacked the 'killer' instinct, and in this they were probably correct, for it is not in the British sporting make-up, and certainly not in rugby football. They ease up, unconsciously, against weaker opponents and this is what they did against the Combined side. Any New Zealand side would have gone on to reach 50 or 60 points. Yet, in the end, it doesn't matter, for there is a wonderful spirit in rugby football and it was always present at Greymouth. The sun shone brightly as we flew over the Southern Alps again to the fair, gentle city of Christchurch, the most English of New Zealand cities, but how un-English is their provincial rugby team which has brought little or no honour to Canterbury in its recent matches against Lions teams.

We had expected Cliff Morgan and Pat Marshall to join the press and T.V. party later on Thursday after our arrival at Christchurch but after settling in to our United Services Hotel headquarters we met Pat but no Cliff, who had been held up, travelling via Johannesburg. Unfortunately Cliff had missed the first French test match at Bloemfontein by a couple of hours owing to a plane delay. He eventually arrived on Friday morning, full of pep and vitality and not, as anticipated, suffering from Doctor Smith's 'circadian dysrhythmia'.

On Thursday evening we chatted with Charles Dick and his family and recalled his fine play for Cambridge and Scotland in the centre. The Scottish Lions in the party met him and I am sure they enjoyed meeting his charming daughter. Friday was a delightfully sunny day in Christchurch, and what a lovely city it is; gentle by nature and, friendly, contrasting so strongly with Canterbury rugby, and like oil and water, they do not appear to blend. What happens to players when they don the red and black jersey of Canterbury? What do the coaches tell them to do? Why do all the other provinces appear to dislike them? How does all this happen in such a polite and gentle city like Christchurch. For me, with Canterbury playing at the Park it resembles all too much the bull rings of the quieter towns in Spain!

Yet the Lions and the accompanying press party did not know what was in store for them on June 21, a match that was to change the whole course and attitude of the tour. Perhaps, it was better that they did not, for many would have said, 'Why bother to play the match. We will not enjoy it and may as well concede it. Let them have a bloodless victory! Friday's papers told us that the Canterbury coaches, Professor Stewart and Morrie Dixon, had prepared their own brand of rugby for the Lions match and studied all the Lions' weaknesses. Presumably, one of the weaknesses must have concerned the noble art of self-defence.

I despatched a cable to the Welsh Brewers on Friday, via Arwyn Owen, in honour of champion club, Bridgend, at the celebration dinner at Bindles, Cold Knap, Barry. The six London Welsh members of the Lions party wished Bridgend well, for it had been a close tussle for the *Western Mail* Championship and the Welsh Brewers do a splendid job each year in providing such an excellent meal. In turn the managing director of the Welsh Brewers, sent a telegram of good wishes to Carwyn James and his Lions, from the dinner.

Barry John withdrew from the Lions' side with slight back trouble and in this he was wise, as were the team management, rather than risk him in what proved to be, as in 1966, a dirty match. As it was, it proved disastrous enough for the Lions even in victory.

>Eleventh Match
>Versus Canterbury at Lancaster Park, Christchurch, June 19.
>Lions won by a goal, two penalties and a try (14) to a penalty (3).
>*Weather:* Sunny. *Ground:* Greasy. *Crowd:* 53,000.
>Teams:
>CANTERBURY: W. F. McCormick; L. Jones, H. T. Joseph, W. D. Cottrell, R. J. Woolhouse; O. D. Bruce, L. J. Davis; A. E. Hopkinson, R. T. Norton, A. McLellan, J. K. Burns, H. H. McDonald, A. E. Mathieson, I. H. Penrose (capt.), A. J. Wyllie.
>BRITISH ISLES: J. P. R. Williams; D. J. Duckham, S. J. Dawes (capt.), A. Lewis, J. C. Bevan; C. M. H. Gibson, G. O. Edwards; R. J. McLoughlin, J. V. Pullin, A. B. Carmichael, W. D. Thomas, W. J. McBride, M. Hipwell, P. J. Dixon, J. F. Slattery.
>*Referee:* Dr H. Rainey (Wellington).

There were fifty thousand in the ground when the teams fielded, and thousands waiting outside. The sun shone brightly and the scene was just perfect but, alas, the Canterbury lamb turned savage at the very first line-out, for as Fergus Slattery was watching the ball move away from the line-out, and was at least twenty yards from it, he received an almighty bash on the mouth from a 'friendly' Canterbury knuckle. That was the start of it! At the first maul, Wyllie, the rugged loose-forward, who could well have lost his test place as a result of his play in this match did some steeplechasing or 'climbing in', which New Zealand officials, referees and players regard as 'legal' play but which in any other country would be classed as 'highly dangerous'.

From the stand, one could not see what was going on in the set scrums but suddenly Sandy Carmichael had to have treatment, and after the next scrum, he was forced to leave the field. What was happening was that Carmichael was being belted in the face and as one Lion forward told me, 'The sound of knuckle against cheek bone was terrible!' Fortunately for the player concerned, we knew that Sandy, one of the cleanest props in the game would not retaliate! He played there all afternoon and took it, and we hope that the 'executioner' is proud of his performance which brought so much glory to Canterbury on that sad day.

At full-back the man who seems to think he is the toughest rugby player in the world, Fergie McCormick can, it would appear, tackle any one he likes but apparently does not like to be tackled himself. He seemed eager to 'cross swords' with everyone and in the second half he entered the line about half a dozen times in order to show 'he could do it' and pull the match out of the fire. Each time he was caught and in the last maul he objected strongly on being given some of his own 'medicine'.

To my mind, there were three main offenders in the Canterbury side and in my opinion the provincial selectors should consider their positions carefully for future matches.

The question one asks is, 'Were they encouraged to play as they did? Were the selectors not well aware of their tendency to play in such a manner? Was not the Canterbury Union condoning "dirty" play by including them? How could the Lions be blamed for creating the atmosphere since all previous matches had been clean and sporting? What special brand of their "own" rugby had the Canterbury coaches, Stewart and Dixon, prepared and should they not shoulder some of the blame for the disgraceful exhibition?'

The tragedy of it all was that if Canterbury had concentrated on playing rugby throughout, they were good enough to have run the Lions to a point or two. They were the losers in every way and what followed brought further disquieting thoughts about New Zealand rugby. Surprisingly enough it came from the mouth of the Chairman of New Zealand Selectors, Ivan Vodanovitch. It was a warning to the Lions that, if they did not get off the ball in the rucks, the first test match at Carisbrooke Park, Dunedin, would resemble the Battle of Passchendaele!

I cannot recall in all my years as a student of the game a more inflammatory and irresponsible statement made by a senior official,

ABOVE: Barry John, architect of a great victory in the First Test, shows his amazing skill as he slips past New Zealand defenders 'like a ghost'. BELOW: John McLauchlan, the brave prop known as 'Mighty Mouse', scores the only try in the First Test, and writes his name in rugby history

RIGHT: At New Plymouth, Taranaki's full back Hill scored one of the best tries of the tour against the Lions, diving over as he was tackled by Chris Rea

BELOW: 'The King' beats the record. Barry John scores a brilliant individual try against New Zealand Universities to create a new record for a tourist in New Zealand, passing Gerry Brand's 1937 total of 100 points for the Springboks

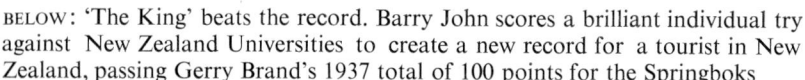

who, until that moment, I had regarded with esteem as a gentleman. What then could have happened to him? Was he driven to it by constant pressure from his colleagues? Did he crack under the strain as the superior skill of the Lions backs threatened, as he and his fellow selectors searched for midfield backs?

As no Lions were injured in rucks against Canterbury but all in the open field, standing up, when they were either punched or kicked, many in the thighs and one in the groin, was it a concerted plan of the three selectors to make this statement, which took New Zealand by storm on Sunday morning, and completely shocked the Lions? If only I could repeat what the Lions thought of Ivan Vodanovitch at that moment, he would retire from the game. Can any British follower imagine Bert Agar or Cliff Jones even suggesting such a course of action 'off the record'? I am sure Fred Allen, Neil McPhail, Arthur Marslin and company blushed with shame when they read it. It was in rugby parlance ... 'the end'!

This statement by Vodanovitch was 'regretted' by the Lions manager and Coach James repudiated the 'validity' of it, as the Lions were taught to stand up in the rucks. This was true, for James was keen about this and had been since the moment of his appointment. Mr Vodanovitch had said the Lions were injured lying on the ball. What rubbish! I have always known, since I first visited the pleasant land of New Zealand that a few officials and players have a hard streak in them ... some Canterbury players far worse than others – and it was Canterbury that caused a brave Lion like Jim Telfer to make his famous speech in 1966. I wonder what he must have said when he read the papers on Sunday June 20, 1971 and saw that Canterbury had been 'at it' again, and had LOST again!

In fairness to Jack Sullivan, the chairman of the New Zealand Council, who had suffered a most difficult time in office and done extremely well, he came out with the statement, as soon as his attention had been drawn to Vodanovitch's 'outburst', that was warmly welcomed at the time, especially by the Lions, for it said, 'There will be no battle at Carisbrooke next Saturday,' and I am sure he meant this, which had to be said.

The *Christchurch Press* one of the best of morning papers in New Zealand, was relatively calm and mild on Monday morning, but came out with the truth on Tuesday morning and published a picture on its back page of the Ground during the match, and headed it with 'That Game of Shame', while rugby writer John Brooks said it is 'Time for Common Sense', and Sports Editor Dick Brittenden said, 'Firm Action by Union Needed'. The London press were quoted and all had given the match and the attitude of Canterbury players much 'stick', while many readers contributed letters expressing disgust and shame. Other papers in New Zealand, include Terry McLean's *New Zealand Herald*, really had 'a go', and this was encouraging for the Lions to some extent, but it could not replace McLoughlin and Carmichael. *Truth* said, 'New Zealand Rugby has become as grotesque as a wounded bull'. How true of Canterbury!

The paper *Truth* went much further than most and named the three 'villains' on the field – but what of those off the field? The men who should, perhaps, have received the greatest 'reprimand', and that from the New Zealand Council, were the two Canterbury coaches, Professor Stewart and Morrie Dixon. A side does not normally play in any special manner in New Zealand unless encouraged to do so and I am still asking myself is the 'stoush' or rough play we saw from Canterbury, the special 'brand' of rugby the coaches said they had in mind? It is a question only they can answer, and perhaps, there is only one answer. How sad for the gentle city of Christchurch.

But enough of the controversy and the thousands of words written about it and, I am glad to say, in unison by the New Zealand and British press. What of the match and its scores? The Lions won it because of their superior back play, their ability to hang on at forward, and their superb cover defence. Edwards and Gibson, under almost constant pressure at half-back, played superbly and the three-quarter line tackled bravely and effectively. Bevan was a tremendous attacker and his try a supreme example of youthful determination. At full-back young John Williams, a musician of some quality and an all round sportsman, stood firm. For him it was 'Verdun' and they did not pass! The Canterbury side just could not score and Williams showed, in striking contrast to McCormick, how enjoyable full-back play can be, even if it is hard.

Canterbury took the lead after 12 minutes with a forty yard penalty by McCormick. The Lions equalised with a twenty yard goal by Gibson after 36 minutes. Before the interval (there were five minutes of stoppages in the first half) Bevan got his wonder try after good approach work by Gibson carried on by Williams and Dawes. Early in the second half Williams kicked a twenty yard penalty and after 26 minutes, in true Welsh 1971 fashion, Edwards, from a scrum, worked a dummy scissors with Gibson on the open side in the Canterbury '25', and Lewis ran at an angle to take the inside pass and crash over for the decisive score. The Lions could not be overtaken and deservedly won the match of Canterbury 'stoush'.

On Sunday afternoon the team flew direct to Blenheim but the press party travelled in the morning via Wellington by service route, having a long enough stay at the capital airport for lunch. Blenheim was sunny and remained delightfully so throughout the three days of our stay, and the Criterion Hotel under manager Jack Randle could not have been kinder. His staff worked hard and it was an excellent lesson in rehabilitation work, for the Lions party left the hotel on Wednesday morning fully recovered from their unhappy experience at Canterbury.

A press conference was held at the Criterion on Sunday afternoon and the Lions management were confronted with the now famous, or infamous, 'Passchendaele' statement and, after this meeting at which all New Zealand journalists present expressed their regret at it and revealed a loyalty to the game, there was a tremendous volley of words from typewriters, with both press groups firing heavy cannons into the Canterbury Stockade and the Vodanovitch headquarters. Having been similarly disgusted at what I had seen on Saturday and read on Sunday, I shared in the attack. It was nothing less that a duty to rugby, a game that has been extremely good and kind to me, as to many other journalists. Whatever differences may have existed in the past, between U.K. and New Zealand journalists, on this issue they were united.

The local cable office, with a staff of three, was bombarded and while only preparing to open from 4 p.m. to 8 p.m., it was in action until 1 a.m., punching through 26,000 words to home and overseas papers. That office deserves a big hand! In the evening, the press gang had a 'sing-song' with Manager Jack Randle giving every encouragement and Carwyn James conducting superbly, while Cliff Morgan played with an appealing friendliness. Tudor James, the modern Todd Jones of the Rhondda, sang beautifully and with James sang *Lend Me your Aid* and other notable ballads, while Morgan, cigarette in the corner of his mouth, moved quietly through the Fizzers' 'Little Farm' repertoire of *Laura, Wonderful World, Some Enchanted Evening,* in which Tudor gave an impression of Rossano Brazzi, and many others. John Williams joined with Gilbert and Sullivan arias and it was great relaxation for all.

The Lions team against the Combined Marlborough/Nelson side included almost all the fit men available but the spirit of the side was good and recovering rapidly from the Saturday while one player told me, 'Reading that statement by Vodanovitch was as good as a team talk for us!' On Monday they trained in the morning and then went round Picton Sound by boat, a delightful trip in the sun, and several players fished during the journey with Mike Roberts topping the day's 'catch' with three dragon fish.

Tuesday, like Sunday and Monday, dawned perfectly with crisp, clear frosty darkness giving way to the hunter of east, and soon the streets were warm and friendly again. A superb climate in Blenheim and extremely friendly people with local N.Z.R.U. Council member Pat Dwyer and his liaison staff, heading the list. The Combined side included one notable All Black forward in Alan Sutherland and the side was led by his elder brother, Ray, while the Combined pack were expected to provide strong opposition.

Twelfth Match
Versus Combined Marlborough and Nelson at Lansdowne Park, Blenhein, June 22.
Lions won by five goals and two tries (31) to four tries (12).
Weather: Sunny. *Ground:* Firm. *Crowd:* 12,400.
Teams:
COMBINED XV: L. C. Sparks; T. W. Mitchell, R. G. Bowater, J. T. Gleeson, G. C. Ross; A. M. Goddard, R. J. May; J. W. Joseph, T. W. Forrest, B. F. Smith, R. P. Dickson, R. S. Sutherland, A. R. Sutherland, B. C. Grant, J. P. Allan.
BRITISH ISLES: R. B. Hiller; T. G. R. Davies, J. S. Spencer, C. W. W. Rea, A. G. Biggar; C. M. H. Gibson (capt.), R. Hopkins; J. McLauchlan. F. A. L. Laidlaw, J. F. Lynch, G. L. Brown, M. G. Roberts, D. L. Quinnell, W. J. McBride, P. J. Dixon.
Referee: Mr R. Fenton (Otago).

Into the Deep South

From the very first whistle this was a pleasant match and, in perfect rugby conditions, provided real entertainment and enjoyment for a record crowd at the ground. Sitting in the sun in the stand one could not but enjoy it and it did much to restore one's faith in the game and in New Zealand rugby, generally, following the 'disaster' of Lancaster Park, Christchurch. The Combined side found the speed and combination of the Lions too much for them in the first half, and Hiller's superb kicking saw four tries converted from the touch-line out of five, and a lead of 23 points to nil at the interval for the tourists.

In the second half the Lions had a low sun in their eyes and a breeze against them which the Combined side exploited cleverly, with low diagonal kicks away from Hiller. Again, as they won greater possession, the Combined side did it frequently and after Biggar had scored his third try after five minutes of the second half for Hiller to convert and increase the lead to 28 points the Combined side countered, much to the delight of a happy crowd that appeared to have no prejudices.

It was difficult at times to understand the rulings of the Referee, Mr Fenton of Otago, who awarded 16 penalties during the match to the Combined side and only two to the Lions. It did not affect the wonderful spirit of the match but it caused one to look northwards and think of Australia! Fortunately, for the Lions, the Combined players had left their kicking boots behind in the dressing room and failed with eleven kicks at goal, including the four conversions, with Sparks missing nine and Alan Sutherland two.

Again, there were two knocks-on in the final Combined try but it did not really matter for the tour had got back on its feet. Rugby was in charge and not a blow thrown or a boot launched in anger or any malice aforethought, which cheered the Lions no end. Another rough match would have finished the tour and the influence of local officials and the excellent captain, Ray Sutherland, was evident, not that the Combined side ever had a reputation for rough play, as they appeared to enjoy their rugby.

In fact, they achieved more than any other side, up to that time, by scoring four tries against the Lions, which was quite remarkable considering the tourists had conceded only five tries in their nine previous matches in New Zealand. It was due to exploitation of local conditions and fast following-up, for the

Lions didn't relax, as acting captain, Mike Gibson, told me 'We just did not get enough ball to keep attacking and somehow, the whistle always appeared to go when we gained possession on the attack, but it was such an enjoyable match, that nobody worried.'

In the first half the Lions got tries through Biggar, Gibson, Dixon, Biggar and Davies, with Hiller converting the first four without any vocal criticism from the crowd. In the second half Biggar got another which Hiller converted and then Rea got one to make the total 31 points. In between these tries the Combined got four through J. P. Allan, R. Sutherland, J. T. Gleeson and A. R. Sutherland.

Gerald Davies got a beauty which probably won him his place in first test team, while Biggar played at his best, thrusting forward with his long stride and looking a real international. Rea had a good game and Gibson again played soundly at outside-half. Spencer was still not at his best and this may have been due to his hamstring which had barely recovered. Laidlaw went through the match after a long absence through knee injury and the two props, Lynch and McLauchlan, had a splendid day, frequently lifting their opposite numbers into the air, and making sure of their test places. Dixon had an excellent match on the flank and McBride appeared to enjoy himself at No. 8 but, once again, Quinnell was unlucky while playing well for he had another accidental kick on his injured knee.

The evening was a happy and gay one with a sing-song after dinner in the dining-room with several of the Combined side joining in. Thanks to Blenheim and its people, and the Combined side plus the sunshine, sanity returned to the Lions tour and it was 'on the road again'.

CHAPTER SIX

The First Test

The Lions were delayed at Blenheim before travelling to Dunedin direct by their charter 'Friendship' while the Press Gang travelled on service routes to Wellington and Christchurch before arriving in Dunedin for a late lunch. The early start at Blenheim, before the sun was up, did not suit everyone and, fortunately, Vivian was helped in his packing by Sandy Carmichael and Willie John McBride. However, they were too efficient and packed almost everything except the 'kitchen sink', and most of the time taken up by the three flights to get from Blenheim to Dunedin, was used in searching for Vivian's international air ticket!

It was wet at Dunedin with the promise of a heavy ground at Carisbrooke Park, and soon after the Lions arrived in the city, the All Blacks mustered at their hotel some 100 yards away. The injured members of the party, Ray McLoughlin, Mick Hipwell, Barry John and Gareth Edwards were there to meet us at the hotel and the Press Gang chatted to them, as the Lions main party had taken lunch at the airport before engaging in one of the hardest training sessions of the tour. Carwyn James did not use footballs in this session, planning to improve the physical approach and get players properly attuned for the test match.

The Lions had two more training sessions on the Thursday and the All Blacks a hard one in the morning, and another one on Friday. During the Thursday session, Gareth Edwards slipped in a pot-hole at the ground and damaged a hamstring muscle, and was forced to leave the field. An examination revealed that he would be a doubtful starter for the Test but the Lions management decided to keep the matter quiet and say that he would play. As events turned out, it was the right decision, and while he spent no more then ten minutes on the field, his able deputy Ray Hopkins played exceedingly well as a substitute and shared in a test triumph.

The Lions had selected their test side round the Welsh Grand

Slam side, with the full Welsh back division except for Gibson, now playing at his best. The backs read... Williams, Davies, Gibson, Dawes, Bevan, John and Edwards. All, except Bevan, had played in New Zealand before and were determined to avenge previous defeats. Three Welshmen were in the pack, which had been selected on a Welsh-Irish basis, and in the original eight it would have been McLoughlin, Pullin, Carmichael, McBride, Thomas, Hipwell, Davies and Taylor. However, for this match it was Lynch, Pullin, McLauchlan, Thomas, McBride, Dixon, Davies and Taylor.

So the side included nine Welshmen. This was a shrewd move, mainly psychological, as they were all playing well, even though Davies at number eight and missed five matches with a serious groin injury resulting from a kick. These Welshmen had suffered two heavy defeats in 1969 and were not considered real international players by New Zealanders when they arrived in 1971. Consequently, they were determined to show that they had much to offer and that the Grand Slam had not been a fortunate win at home.

Senior Irish internationals, McBride and Gibson, Lions of considerable experience, wanted to show the New Zealanders that they, too, were outstanding players, and that the loss of their close friend and outstanding prop, Ray McLoughlin, could be made good.

Lynch replaced his team mate as did 'Ian' McClauchlan, and they were equally determined to prove themselves as good as the first choice players. Pullin was always the quiet, steady worker as hooker, and there were no fears that he would not do a good job of work, if he had the 'weight' and the shove that the Lions had acquired through diligent practice. Dixon came in to replace the injured Mick Hipwell who was suffering from fluid on the knee. Hipwell wanted to wait until Saturday morning, before having the fluid withdrawn, so keen was he to share in the struggle, but he did not realise then that he had played his last match of the tour.

'Little John' Taylor won the other flank position because of his speed over the ground and his good hands, and thus he had proved himself, after all at home had said he would be too small! However, now he had been selected there was still much for him to do to convince the school of thought that wanted all flankers to be the size of Ian Kirkpatrick!

As the city prepared for the match I chatted to many senior experts including Charles Saxton, Victor Cavanagh, Jack Manchester, Douglas Hamilton, Tubby Woodhouse and the most helpful secretary of the Otago Union, Bert Sincock. The attendance was expected to be a record one, despite the threat of rain, and there were no late withdrawals on Friday night to disturb the pre-match preparations. The three All Blacks selectors were seen out for a brisk afternoon walk and despite many team talks at Wain's Hotel, the All Blacks headquarters, all was peaceful, and gradually the threat of 'Passchendaele' passed. Poor Ivan Vodanovitch must have regretted using the word, for even he, at this stage, must have realised that rugby football is only a game!

Both sides were wary of the other and made their forecasts cautiously. The local radio programme was interrupted every 15 minutes or so to give the latest reports on training or forecasts, while Cliff Morgan was interviewed about half a dozen times. Everyone had his say; opinion was divided, but on Friday night it appeared as if the All Blacks were slight favourites. They had picked a strong side, although forced to make a change on Tuesday because Otago's prop, strong man Keith Murdoch, had once again failed to make it against the Lions through injury.

Saturday dawned clear after a night of heavy showers, and a stiff breeze, aided by the sun, got to work on drying out Carisbrooke Park. At 4.0 a.m. in the morning I had been awakened by a call from my assistant editor, Rex Reynolds in Cardiff, asking me, with suitable amusing apologies, to lay on a telephone call at end of the match and phone immediately enough comment, off the cuff, to launch a special edition of the *Western Mail!* After protesting vigorously in the dark that I was full of penicillin (as Doctor Smith had given me a 'shot' late on Friday night for a poisoned foot), I promised to do what I could and ring him back at a more civilised hour! However, I did get up earlier than usual and set off for Carisbrooke Park where Bert Sincock came to my aid and allowed me to use his private phone for 'five minutes' immediately after the match.

This was a great break because a week-end in New Zealand is a 'lost' one, as far as work is concerned, except for the efficient telegraph cabling system, and there was no chance of having a phone put in on Saturday morning. This, of course, could be true of the UK nowadays, but Mr Sincock, bless him, enabled the *Western Mail* to have a 6.0 a.m. edition highlighting the first rugby test of 1971 and keeping the most devoted of Welsh readers contented!

Thirteenth Match
Versus New Zealand (First Test) at Carisbrooke Park, Dunedin on June 26th, 1971
Won by the Lions by two penalties and a try (9) to a penalty (3).
Weather: Sunny. *Ground:* Greasy. *Crowd:* 45,000.
Teams:
NEW ZEALAND: W. F. McCormick; B. A. Hunter, B. G. Williams, W. D. Cottrell, K. R. Carrington; R. E. Burgess, S. M. Going; B. L. Muller, R. W. Norton, R. A. Guy, C. E. Meads (capt), P. J. Whiting, A. M. McNaughton, A. R. Sutherland, I. A. Kirkpatrick.
BRITISH ISLES: J. P. R. Williams; T. G. R. Davies, C. M. H. Gibson, S. J. Dawes (capt), J. C. Bevan; B. John, G. O. Edwards; J. McLauchlan, J. V. Pullin, J. F. Lynch, W. D. Thomas, W. J. McBride, P. J. Dixon, T. M. Davies and J. Taylor.
Referee: Mr J. C. Pring (Auckland).

Carisbrooke Park was an impressive sight when the teams fielded together to the swirl of the Pipe Band, for there were 45,000 spectators packed inside the ground and about five thousand more on the railway line and road above the town end of the ground. Before Bob Irvine and myself went on the air for NZBC, a policewoman came to the box asking that an appeal be put out warning those 'tresspassers' on the railway line that the 'Southerner' Express would be passing by at 3.0 p.m. and that it would proceed slowly, whistling loudly, and that the line would have to be cleared. This famous bank at Dunedin is known as the 'Scotsman's Stand' and is always well patronised on international or test match days.

The weather was sunny and bright and the Brass Band played the National Anthem before Barry John kicked off for the British Isles into the breeze and the sun. For the next ten minutes we saw New Zealand forward play at its best in a series of menacing attacks that stretched the Lions to the limit. Still, they held on bravely, and even attacked themselves, forcing the All Blacks to 'carry over' and a scrum five was ordered with the Lions' put in.

The Lions won the ball and Edwards went blind. He was tackled by McCormick and held up outside the line. He further aggravated his injury as he fell and the play was stopped. Edwards was spoken to by his captain and then led from the field. As he jogged off, Hopkins started undressing and soon took his place. Almost immediately the Lions were awarded a penalty at a line-out and John attempted the first kick at goal of the match but he was just wide.

The All Blacks soon attacked again and Going and Burgess were dangerous in turn before Burgess attempted a drop at goal and Bevan cleared. The Lions got down into the All Blacks twenty-five where they moved the ball to the left but could not get clear. There was then a lapse in the All Blacks' defence; Sutherland had a clearing kick charged down, and 'Ian' McLauchlan burst through between two defenders to win the touch down as the ball bounced away, over the All Blacks' line.

The 'mighty mouse' had scored, and although the three points were against the run of play they served to boost the Lions who, since the first whistle, had spent most of the time defending, albeit bravely. For once Barry John failed with the conversion attempt but the Lions were in the lead, although one anticipated further menacing onslaughts from the All Blacks with Meads in the van. They were producing good combined rugby and it required the best and bravest of tackles and saves to keep them at bay. It was fascinating to watch, and admirable in spirit, even though it was desperately hard.

McCormick had his first attempt at a penalty goal from 50 yards but was short and John cleared. Then followed an award against the Lions in their own '25'. Surely Fergus McCormick, who was not having a happy day at full-back, would not miss this one, after the Lions had been adjudged off-side at a short penalty for not retiring. However, miss it he did, and the groan could be heard as far south as Invercargill. However he received yet another chance of levelling the scores in injury time before the whistle went for half time.

John Dawes was trapped the wrong side of the maul and although trying to get away from the ball and the feet, he was penalised. McCormick succeeded in kicking the goal with his third attempt, to be cheered to the echo by a crowd that was unashamedly partisan but nevertheless friendly and sporting. The All Blacks were almost in for a try as the whistle went for half-time and the Lions themselves must have been grateful for the rest and, indeed, encouraged that they had held a strong All Blacks side, playing well, in the first half.

More important, the Lions had held their own in the set scrums; refusing to be pushed back in the rucks, although the All Blacks had won more of the ball in this phase, and had allowed no gaps in the loose. They had not been able to win enough ball themselves at the line-out especially at 5, 6 and 7, but they had slowed down the momentum of the peels-off round the end of the line-out. They had tackled valiantly and backs and forwards had gone down, taking an opponent with them, and they had gone low for there was no high tackle offered to invite the inevitable hand off. Again, young Hopkins, appearing as a substitute to win his first test cap, as he had done his first international cap, for an injured Edwards, was proving a sound reliable player.

Early in the second half John dropped for goal but was wide and there was a moment of doubt for all in the British camp, that he could have lost his fine sense of kicking accuracy. Again, he slipped on the greasy surface when attempting a side step and was smothered by All Black jerseys. He required attention from the faithful St John's Ambulance men and, shortly afterwards, the magic sponge was called for again. Yet he survived and soon sent a wonderful punt spinning down towards the left corner to gain a valuable attacking touch. Gerald Davies was then put away down the right touch-line and when hemmed in, kicked on and chased, only to miss a try by inches as the ball rolled away into touch in goal. After 16 minutes of the second half the All Blacks fell off-side and John placed the ball 30 yards out. He trotted up, kicked, and over went the ball for the Lions to regain the lead.

It was a vital kick as the lead boosted the Lions' spirit and made them even more determined to hold on, for great was the prize if victory could be achieved. The Lions were better now; more confident, and Bevan went near to scoring on the left wing, chasing a kick over the line. There was an obstruction on John Taylor and Barry John attempted a shot at goal from 50 yards, just a shade outside his normal distance, and the ball sailed to the left of the uprights.

Back came the All Blacks with a series of menacing raids to

exert constant pressure on the Lions but they stood firm. Time and time again John drove the enemy back with superb touch finders from within his own '25' as the All Blacks fought magnificently to get level again. However, try as they did they just could not do it. Williams and McCormick served as battering rams, as rucks were won and the direction of the attack switched, but it was always Hopkins to John, and John sending them back, twice with the aid of useful penalty awards. After 28 minutes of the second half McCormick had the chance of a lifetime to put his side level with a penalty attempt from 23 yards but, alas for NZ he failed again!

It was desperately exciting for all, and tiring – almost as tiring watching as it was playing. Yet the thin brave red line of British defenders could not be broken and the wraith-like John, shimmering in and out of the black jerseyed raiders, sent the ball back over the heads of oncoming forwards; turning them and frustrating them at the same time. The clock appeared to move round all too slowly for British eyes, but much too quickly for those of New Zealand! Barry John and John Dawes chatted away to each other and Hopkins was as brave as two men in face of the big strong and sporting All Blacks pack. Could the Lions hold out or would New Zealand get a try and McCormick kick a winning conversion?

The crowd were full of applause for British guts and tenacity but they wanted their heroes to snatch the match out of the fire. Then, suddenly, flank forward McNaughton got to John and grabbed his jersey collar as the Lion got rid of the ball. McNaughton swung him round to the ground without malice, but it was a late tackle, and Referee Pring, who had controlled admirably, had no alternative but to award a penalty 36 yards out, against New Zealand. It was decisive!

John gathered the ball – put it down – stepped back – and in a silence that almost made one shiver with anxiety, he trotted up and bang, over she went...a goal! It was 9–3 and the Lions could hardly lose! The All Blacks gathered themselves for a last effort in the closing minutes but even they must have felt it was too late. Gerald Davies made a good mark to stop one attack and then came another, but the Lions held firm and when the last whistle was sounded by Referee Pring, to end a splendid match that was a credit to both sides, several of the Lions jumped in the air with both joy and relief! Objective Number One had been achieved. After an interval of 12 years a British side had defeated New Zealand in a test match at home.

The Lions rushed to the entrance to the dressing rooms and lined up to applaud Colin Meads and his team as they left the field and the crowd surged round. In the commentary box, I chatted away to New Zealand and the British Isles, and subdued my personal excitement and obvious pleasure in an attempt to provide a fair summary of the play. Then a quick dash to Secretary Sincock's office and a long chat to Cardiff as Bill Hook took the copy, at his usual quick speed, and Alan Wood subbed it to send it down for setting. At least the 6.0 a.m. Special Edition of the *Western Mail* would have something good to say. Well done, the Lions!

I typed the *Echo* story, not quite believing it had all happened, and pinching myself, occasionally, just to make sure I was not dreaming. New Zealanders shook hands warmly and said, 'Well done!', and they meant what they said. The sad memories of 1959 had been erased. This was a match of quality; of no doubtful decisions, a match of chances taken and chances missed, and the Lions had won. Manager Smith was at the entrance to the dressing room tunnel, and he hugged each player in turn with the tears not far from his eyes. Who could blame him, had he cried a little with joy? For him and his party, especially, it was a moment of triumph and truth and for those of us, who had travelled the world, optimistically, in search of triumph, it was a special moment... one like the five faces on the old bars of Fry's milk chocolate... but particularly the one of realisation!

Manager Smith recovered quickly from a natural but rare show of emotion and said, 'I am deeply proud of the Lions today. Everyone was a hero in a magnificent match that was a victory for rugby football. The All Blacks were a fine side and played really well and we are all proud to have beaten them and proud to be British. I cannot praise too highly the work of Carwyn James as coach and John Dawes as captain and the way in which all the party has worked for this day.'

Carwyn James was highly delighted, of course, and told me, 'It is the victory that makes all the hard work worth-while and our preparations at home and hard work out here have been justified. The All Blacks played really well. They are a good side and we are proud to have beaten them. Gareth Edwards was doubtful and we did not know how long he would last but we wanted to start with our best side. Yet, when he went off with further hamstring trouble, Chico Hopkins played really well. He did a fine job to share in the victory and all the players tackled well and covered superbly. Now we really have a chance of the series!'

The New Zealand captain, Colin Meads, was equally sincere, I feel, when he said, 'The better side won, for the Lions took their chances and while we had our opportunities we just could not take them. Still we'll be back and there are three tests to go. I hope the next three games will be as good as this one, for it was played in excellent spirit, but we can do better next time and we will play the same way, only better!'

The British Press threw a champagne party before dinner for the Lions, back at the Southern Cross Hotel and it set the pace for the players to celebrate until the early hours of the morning. The official Test Match dinner went quite well but, sadly, because of work, several of the Press Gang could not attend. Yet on Sunday morning, as the telegrams of congratulation poured in, there was satisfaction at the victory, deservedly gained; admiration for the spirit of approach of the All Blacks, and a modesty that compelled all to admit... 'There's still a long way to go in the series!'

Manager Smith gave a private champagne party before we set off for Queenstown and the Welsh Press 'mafia' flew over the beautiful mountains of Otago to the delightfully attractive resort of Queenstown on the shore of Lake Wakatipu, in an eight-seater plane, swinging round the mountains and along the valleys, just like the superb opening sequence in the *Sound of Music* film. It was a fitting reward for the hard work of the previous day as I sat in the back seat and analysed how the Lions had achieved victory.

There were three vital factors. Foremost of these must be the belated but successful adoption in the British Isles of the system for coaching national sides and eliminating the 'scratch team' approach. Secondly, there was the disciplined control of the 'iron fist in the velvet glove' of the team management, plus the shrewd and skilful coaching and captaincy of Carwyn James and John Dawes; and thirdly, the remarkable team spirit that harnessed the gifted individual skills and determination in the side.

True, the rub of the green was with the Lions in this match, as it had been against them in 1959. It was the Lions who kicked the two vital penalties and the All Blacks who had missed two. Again, it was the Lions who had the decisive and most influential player, tactically, in Barry John. His fine kicking, placed with pin-point accuracy, did more than anything else to win the match by supporting a never-say-die pack of forwards, and raising seige after seige of the British lines. Yet all fifteen players had their moment of glory; one they will never forget!

It was important, too, for rugby football that New Zealand, players, officials and supporters, but especially the Press, took the defeat so well. There was no feeling of sour grapes, if one of disappointment, and the tour was truly 'back on the road'. The greatest show on earth, as far as New Zealand was concerned, was an exciting success and the prospect of a thrilling series, even brighter!

Queenstown was beautiful on arrival with the snow-capped mountains flashing in the bright afternoon sunshine but the next day, a relaxation day, saw continuous rain. The Welsh 'mafia' bravely travelled in the Gondola Sky lift to the café at the top and once there, rang down for all available Lions to make the 'moonshot' lift. It amazed some, delighted others, and even frightened some, but was good value and a memory to savour, as much as the test victory would become a moment to savour in restrospect.

On Tuesday we drove by car down to Invercargill, the southernmost city in the Commonwealth, and it was an excellent trip in dry sunny weather. On the way we lunched with Carwyn James and Terry McLean; a mellow Terry even in the hour of his country's test defeat. Invercargill was cold but the welcome warm and the sun shone brightly. I addressed Southland H.S.O.B. Club and the 250 members present appeared to enjoy it as much as I did, for there is nothing quite like talking rugby to rugby men in the wake of a test victory!

The Lions were still unbeaten in New Zealand at this stage, but memories of the 1966 defeat at Invercargill, which changed the whole course of that tour, following a successful rampage through Australia, remained fresh in the minds of the 'faithful'. Would history repeat itself? There was no mood of over-confidence, and the Lions took no chances, fielding nine of their test players, including Barry John. It was necessary to win, and

Papers from home. The author shows Welsh members of the party some copies of the *Western Mail*, with its full coverage of the tour. Lions, at Greymouth, are Gareth Edwards, Carwyn James, John Bevan and Gerald Davies

Off duty! John Dawes golfing – and searching for the ball. John Taylor has no such problems

The Master Fisherman, Mike Roberts, with his Dargon Fish at Picton Sound

The Second Test. Sid Going, the All Black scrum-half and 'man of the match', getting his pass away as John Taylor comes in to tackle

Gareth Edwards under pressure in the Second Test. Muller and Norton come through the line-out on to Edwards as he prepares to clear to touch

win well to lay another 'bogy', if only to give satisfaction to those Lions who were not as fortunate in the South Island in 1966.

Fourteenth Match
Versus Southland at Rugby Park, Invercargill, June 30th, 1971.
Won by the Lions by five goals (25) to one penalty (3).
Weather: Sunny. *Ground:* Greasy and holding. *Crowd:* 22,000.
Teams:
SOUTHLAND: D. Nichol; R. Hardie, M. Michell, B. Small, L. Booth; J. Polson, D. Langford; I. Gutsell, K. McRae, I. McKenzie, G. McAllister, G. Dermody (capt), H. Miller, R. Kingdon, K. Stewart.
BRITISH ISLES: J. P. R. Williams; T. G. R. Davies, J. S. Spencer, S. J. Dawes (capt), A. C. Biggar; B. John, R. Hopkins; C. B. Stevens, J. V. Pullin, J. F. Lynch, G. L. Brown, W. D. Thomas, J. Taylor, T. M. Davies, J. F. Slattery.
Referee: Mr A. F. Gurnsey (Canterbury).

This match did not prove to be as spectacular as the Test, and one could not expect another exciting cliff-hanger, for the Lions proved far too strong and clever for the Southlanders who were not quite as strong as they were in 1966, 1959 or 1950. The forwards battled away hard, and sometimes vigorously, and a good right hook was planted on the side of the head of Ray Hopkins, that laid him out for the count of ten! However, they could never contain a Lions' pack that set out to win the ball.

This they did and the backs, though not moving with the same speed and elan as on some of the dry grounds experienced, scored valuable tries and Barry 'the King' John produced five superb conversions to improve all tries scored. In so doing, John passed the century mark for points on the tour, and brought his New Zealand total to 94, well within striking distance of the record 100 points created by Springbok fullback, Gerry Brand, in 1937. John found the marking on the greasy ground, which reduced his mobility a little, much sterner than in most places but his kicking was superb. Whether converting from the touchline or kicking the roller into touch, he was amazingly accurate.

Southland took the lead after 13 minutes when their excellent and sound left-footed full-back, Nichol, landed a 25 yard penalty. The Lions, however, took the lead, which they were not to lose, three minutes later. The ball came back for the Lions to move left and John, running on, cut out centres Spencer and Dawes, and handed straight on to John Williams, joining the line. The full-back handed on to Biggar in full flight and he turned inside, shook off a tackle and crashed over for a good wing's try. John converted from near the touch-line but the Lions had to wait another seventeen minutes before they increased their lead.

During Lions pressure on the Southland '25' Mervyn Davies went away from a line-out and handed on to Slattery who made ground and then Taylor finished off for a first class back row try that John again converted. Before the interval Delme Thomas, jumping well at no. 3., tapped down straight to left wing, Biggar, who moved inside and then out again to dodge over cleverly and John kicked the goal, again from the touch-line, making the score 15–3 at the interval.

In the second half the Lions tended to over-elaborate, and set-up Spencer as a second phase McRea, but Southland defended well and 23 minutes of the second half passed before the fourth try came. Biggar ran into a movement moving left to surprise the defence and then turned inside again to hand on to Dawes, and his captain dodged over cleverly for John to convert.

The last and fifth try was possibly the best of the day. The Lions went first left and the ball was rucked quickly for Gerald Davies to move right and find Williams able to support him on the right touch-line. The full-back galloped away and then sent inside to the fleet-footed Taylor, who handed inside again to Stack Stevens, making an admirable first appearance as prop, and inside again was the ubiquitous number eight, now a player of world class, Mervyn Davies, to take the final high pass out of the sun and dive over at the posts. John kicked the goal and the final minutes were important only for McBride substituting for an injured Brown with shoulder trouble that proved to be severe bruising.

The win at Invercargill was pleasing, although Earle Reed of NZPA called it a 'ragged game', for it was the biggest win achieved there by a Lions' side and Barry John reached a century of points for the tour which was no mean achievement in eight matches. This modest young man was rapidly becoming the 'rugby writers' dream' since he rarely, if ever, failed to supply something of interest on the tour, even if one was forced to check the reference books thoroughly after each of his many fine performances, in case he had superceded one record or another.

With the passing of each day, the title of 'King John' became more secure and everyone paid homage to the 'King', while he was to remain a law unto himself on the field, despite a close understanding with his captain, John Dawes. This exceptional touch of rugby genius, for that is what it was on this tour, lifted the Lions to the pinnacle, time upon time, to the delight of all, even those who watched in support of their own sides. New Zealanders were not full of praise for the Lions after this match, although one did write that 'John once again was the star turn', since the long run had produced in them, perhaps sub-consciously and not unexpectedly, an over-critical eye.

The Southland forwards played with enthusiasm and vigour, and none better than the 18-year-old loose forward, Ken Stewart, in his first year out of Otago Boys High School. The burly Southland captain, Dermody, who was on the winning side in 1966, played well as did the full-back, Nichol. The Lions enjoyed their stay in sunny Invercargill and wished it had been longer but, on Thursday morning, the 'show was on the road' again heading for New Plymouth.

The team travelled by charter 'Friendship' in one hop, while the Press had to fly by normal service routes, yet this was made more pleasant for us by Captain Cadwallader, flying the service 'Friendship' from Invercargill to Christchurch, as he flew over all the beauty sports, including Queenstown and Coronet Peak, on the way. Vivian and myself thanked him for his kindness and met him later at various airports. Perhaps, it is timely to pay tribute to the excellent 'driving' of NAC pilots and the friendliness of their cabin staffs.

New Plymouth is situated in the shadow of the beautiful Mount Egmont, and as we arrived in the dark, we did not see the mountain in all its glory until Sunday, which was a perfect day when we left. It was shrouded in mist and rain on Friday and made only short appearances on Saturday, but on Sunday it was perfect as we flew to Wellington. They have a saying in Taranaki that when you see Mount Egmont it is going to rain and when you cannot see it, it is raining! Anyway the rich dairy farming area needs the rain and the lush green grass produces delicious cream, butter, milk and cheese, as well as powerful, hard working, robust forwards, including the heaviest man in the New Zealand side, prop Brian Muller.

We were billeted in the West Town Motel, adjacent to Rugby Park. The food was excellent and the rooms most comfortable. The Press had to 'double up' and share rooms and normally this would not be difficult but travelling pressmen like to work on their own, and that is why they always ask for single rooms. In fairness to the Union Steamship Company, through Peter Leighton, we did have single rooms in most places, but some of the smaller places experienced difficulty, as one would also expect to find in similar sized towns in the UK.

The Taranaki Rugby Union staged a big reception, regarded by the Lions as one of the best of the tour in the provinces. Noel Stanley, Jim Peacock and George Bowen and press liaison Roger Urbahn were active officials. It was unfortunate that it should have rained hard following a practice on Friday morning, but fortunate that it cleared on Saturday morning to leave conditions reasonably good for the match, even if the surface was greasy. Rugby Park believes it can hold 50,000, but this appears wishful thinking on the part of local officials in the hope that they can 'lift' the test from Dunedin at some future date. The ground appears capable of forty to forty-five thousand (if that) and with only 30,000 for this Lions match it looked full enough. The local record was estimated at 36,000 and I would be inclined to say 40,000 maximum!

Fifteenth Match
Versus Taranaki at Rugby Park, New Plymouth, July 3rd, 1971.
Lions won by one goal, two dropped goals and a penalty (14) to a penalty and two tries (9).
Weather: Dull, dry. *Ground:* Softish. *Crowd:* 30,000.
Teams:
TARANAKI: F. Hill; M. Kidd, G. Neilson, W. Currey, D. Vesty; P. Martin, D. J. Wards; A. Gardiner, F. Harris, B. L. Muller, A. E. Smith, I. Eliason, M. Willis (capt), R. Feather, A. Scown.
BRITISH ISLES: R. B. Hiller; J. C. Bevan, C. W. Rea, A. J. Lewis, D. J. Duckham; C. M. H. Gibson, R. Hopkins; J. McLauchlan, F. L. Laidlaw, J. F. Lynch, G. J. Evans, W. J. McBride, P. J. Dixon, T. M. Davies, J. F. Slattery.
Referee: Mr L. Gibson (Poverty Bay).

The First Test

Taranaki had first fielded a side against a touring team in 1885 and first met a full Lions side in 1904, in a pointless draw. Since that memorable day, they have always provided Lions' sides with vigorous opposition, except possibly in 1930 when they lost 23-7. However, the 1959 and 1966 sides found it hard going against sides with considerable vigour in front, and so the 1971 Lions were well prepared for a hard match in front.

From the first whistle the Taranaki forwards, led by Smith, played extremely well and gave the Lions no respite with four 'up and unders', hotly pursued, in the first three minutes! It reminded me of the song, *When it rains, it rains*.... as the Taranaki forwards came rushing in to crack down the tackler, perfectly fairly, and ruck for the ball. Gibson and Hiller had to make brave marks to save the situation and for a period the Lions looked extremely ragged, but after seven minutes they took the lead because they were geared as always, even against the run of play, to take their chances.

Full-back Hill fielded near his own line but instead of kicking to touch, he kicked out into the field and Hiller, a quick thinker at all time, gathered 45 yards out and dropped high for goal. Over went the ball and three points were placed on the board but Taranaki could not be denied, as they kept up the pressure at forward and harassed the Lions' defence. They moved left, were stopped, but rucked the ball and then went right again from the Lions '25' with the overlap and Hill was in the line to take the pass and dive over for an excellent try. Unfortunately, he could not convert his own try and, this missed kick, together with others was to cost Taranaki the match.

Next it was the turn of the Lions to move in attack and their reward was a fine touring team try. The sharp Hopkins moved away from a scrum and kicked on to the full-back. Hill failed to clear, and Hopkins had it again to put Slattery away, the flanker ran hard for Evans to join in and, finally, Davies crashed over for a try that Hiller did well to convert, leaving the score at 8-3. Hiller and Willis kicked wide with penalty attempts for their respective sides before Bevan was put away and kicked on, only to see the ball go 'dead'. Lewis worked the dummy scissors with Gibson and got over the line but couldn't ground the ball. The Lions pressed hard but their attacks were rather obvious and the Taranaki defence stood firm. Suddenly there was a rush of scoring before the interval and at half-time it looked as if the Lions would move away in the second half although the first half score flattered them.

Gibson was late-tackled after 33 minutes play and from where the ball landed, after the kick, Hiller kicked a 25 yards penalty. Two minutes later Taranaki scored another fine try, one of the best against the Lions up to that time. Hill came up into the attack and kicked high for the Taranaki forwards to arrive with it and overpower the unlucky defender, then ruck the ball for Wards to feed Currey. He sent an overhead pass to Vesty who dived over in the right corner but Hill could not convert. Before the interval the Lions pressed again and from a five yard scrum Hopkins sent it back to Gibson who dropped a straight 25 yard goal.

The Lions had enjoyed the assistance of a fair breeze in the first half but now they had to face it and a Taranaki pack that still held a full head of steam! The Lions still did not play smoothly behind as the second half developed and their forwards were busily engaged trying to hold their own in front. However Taranaki did not vary their play enough while achieving good possession, continuing to place their hopes in the old fashioned 'up and under'. After 11 minutes their efforts were rewarded, for Martin was obstructed after a kick and from where the ball landed, Hill placed a good 37 yard goal.

This ended the scoring but first Evans, in his initial match of the tour, had to leave the field with a nasty cut under his right eye, caused by a clash of heads, and be replaced by Roberts, while Smith of Taranaki, jumping high for the ball, fell awkwardly to tear a ligament in his left knee and be replaced by Paki Paki after 25 minutes.

Smith, one of the unluckiest of forwards, was bidding to get back into the New Zealand test side but this put him out for the rest of the season and was exceptionally painful. Until the end the Lions were under pressure and Hiller and Hopkins made some brave marks. When the tourists did break away and attack, they lacked cohesion and there was far too much kicking, by Hopkins, Gibson and Lewis, and the wings were starved of possession.

The Lions were indeed fortunate to hold out, for Taranaki were deserving of a draw but through good fortune and a good defence, the tourists survived and retained their unbeaten record. Indeed, Hiller went near to increasing their lead with a penalty attempt but the honours of the day went to the Taranaki forwards – as good a pack as the Lions had met up to that time.

On Sunday the caravan moved on... to Wellington... still unbeaten... and the Press Gang received cables to 'send more copy'. The Lions were hitting the headlines at home!

CHAPTER SEVEN

The Second Test

It was a pleasant flight from New Plymouth to Wellington on Sunday morning in glorious sunshine, with the snow-capped Mount Egmont sparkling in many colours. The rich plains below revealed the wealth of New Zealand, with its green lush grass, and one felt that whatever happened over E.E.C., and the terms appeared more favourable to New Zealand at this stage than was anticipated, New Zealand would survive, and Mr Marshall would become something of a hero. At this stage, unfortunately, the nation was not prepared to put him above Colin Meads, but he had done much more to ensure the future of the lovely land of the Two Islands! Yet as one looked down, one realised that New Zealanders, come what may, even if they all had to wear mini skirts, would not starve. They could always live well, off the land!

There was plenty of work to do and letters to write on arrival at Wellington, as soon as one had settled into the comfortable Hotel St George, although the Lions went to the Town Hall to attend the special reception given to them by the Wellington Rugby Supporters' Club headed by Dick Evans. It lasted from 2 p.m. to 6.30 p.m., and included just about everything, but the Lions appeared to enjoy it despite its distinctly Welsh flavour. The Maori concert party provided a pleasant change from routine, while W. J. 'Billy' Wallace, king of New Zealand All Blacks, was introduced to the audience; at 93 years of age and was in quite remarkable form.

The Lions trained hard on Monday in readiness for the Tuesday match against the Varsities and in the evening attended a reception given in their honour by Her Majestys' High Commissioner in New Zealand, Sir Arthur Galsworthy and Lady Galsworthy, at their official residence. This was an enjoyable break and during the day I chatted to W. H. 'Bill' Clark and other New Zealand Universities officials, who were keen to see their side take the Lions record with running rugby!

ABOVE: The Second Test. Ian Kirkpatrick using the shoulder of Mervyn Davies as an aid to jump in the line-out—incidentally keeping Davies earthbound! BELOW: The unhappy match v. Hawkes Bay was marked by brilliant play from the Lions right wing, Gerald Davies, who scored four superb tries. Here he crosses for one of them after leaving defenders prostrate on the ground

The Coach. A fine study of Carwyn James, emphasising a point to his forwards during a training session

The Captain, John Dawes

Gareth Edwards teaching a bashful stone maiden how to pass, outside the team hotel in Brisbane

At the reception it was interesting to chat to the wives of leading New Zealand rugby officials, as they are not often seen in public (this is true of officials' wives everywhere and indeed the wives of the travelling press!). The wives of Messrs Blazey, Morrison and Vodanovitch, appeared just as interested, and almost as knowledgeable as their husbands, and I have it on good authority that New Zealand Selectors' wives have often made a better job of it than their husbands, during their telephone selection sessions. At least, that is what some of the former selectors told me!

There had been a weather forecast for rain for the Tuesday but the day remained dry if somewhat threatening until after the match and there was a late rush to the ground with Neville Lodge providing an apt cartoon of Wellington offices being denuded of workers during the afternoon. An excellent sports cartoonist, with a love of model railways and a former P.O.W., he had some wonderful tales to tell me of travel by taxi in South Africa, but especially in Kimberley. There a taxi driver thought it was rather too far to convey Mr Lodge to a motel three miles from the railway station!

Sixteenth Match
Versus New Zealand Universities at Athletic Park, Wellington, July 6.
Lions won by three goals, three penalties and one dropped goal (27) to two tries (6).
Weather: Dry. *Crowd:* 30,000. *Ground:* Reasonably dry.
Teams:
NEW ZEALAND UNIVERSITIES: E. Taylor; M. P. Collins, H. T. Joseph, G. K. Kember (capt.), D. L. Palmer; R. E. Burgess, R. M. Barlow; P. A. Lindesay, P. Barrett, A. McLellan, R. Lockwood, J. Sherlock, A. Matheson, G. McGee, R. T. De Cleene.
BRITISH ISLES: J. P. R. Williams; D. J. Duckham, S. J. Dawes (capt.), C. M. H. Gibson, J. C. Bevan; B. John, R. Hopkins; J. McLauchlan, F. A. L. Laidlaw, C. B. Stevens, W. D. Thomas, G. L. Brown, J. Taylor, T. M. Davies, J. F. Slattery.
Referee: Mr B. M. Dawson (Southland).

In New Zealand the combined universities' sides contain past and present students, with special emphasis upon the past! Some of the players were professional men aged 28 and 29 years respectively and Joseph, selected on the previous Sunday as an All Black for the Second Test, was a journalist in Christchurch doing an external degree! There is no hard and fast rule on this, as past students play for the Southern Universities in Capetown against touring teams. In the British Isles the various University sides are composed ONLY of students in residence which is better because, although it may not produce sides as strong as overseas countries, it does give young players a chance to represent their universities while in residence.

However, the approach of universities rugby in New Zealand is excellent, and they try to play attractive, open and effective football at all times. In this match they contributed much and scored two splendid tries and it was fitting that their captain, Kember, All Black second five eighth and utility back on two tours, should emphasise the point that his team enjoyed playing against the Lions because they had the same idea as to how the game of rugby football should be played. He suggested that all teams in New Zealand should play the same way and although this statement might not have been popular with the N.Z.R.U. officials and councillors present, Kember was both brave and wise to make it.

If all rugby in New Zealand was played in the spirit of this match, and indeed that of the first two tests, there would be no reason to fear the challenge of soccer. Both sides produced free open rugby and while they made errors they provided a brilliant array of skills for the large mid-week crowd of thirty thousand, which included many schoolboys, and one must pay tribute to the Varsities who were a far better and stronger side than the final score of 27 points to 6 indicated. They had sound basic skills, mobility, and a desire to create something behind, for rugby football is a far more important exercise than mere winning. There is need to employ all fifteen players to their full potential.

Kember was determined, as was the new-look Meads in the First Test, to keep the ball moving and, as the new touch kicking law outside the '25's' encourages players to run, the universities were determined from the start. Their forwards were clever at the line-out and while they jumped they also employed the 'step across' so strongly criticised by New Zealander writer, Gabe

David, after the South African tour of 1970. One assumes this 'step across', which is effective, has put Delme Thomas on his backside more frequently than any other visiting line-out jumper, and saw him knocked out again from the number two and three positions at the line-out. Yet when he changed over with Gordon Brown to jump at five and six, the Lions got more ball.

Yet, well though the Varsities played in this match, they did not have a Barry John, who as 'king' decided that he would beat a few existing records, and one in particular that had stood the test of time for 34 years. In 1937 one of the game's outstanding full-backs and place kickers, Gerry Brand, scored exactly 100 points while on tour in New Zealand with the greatest Springbok side of all time and, incidentally, the only other visiting team to win a full test series in New Zealand.

John started off with two penalty goals to equal Brand's mighty effort and then seven minutes from the interval, received from a scrum while standing on the Varsities '25' line. He 'dummied' to drop at goal and then to swing a pass out to his three-quarter line, before setting off for the goal line. The Varsities' flanker, Matheson, is reported to have said, 'John just rolled his eyes and I fell over!' but John swerved and side-stepped through the Varsities side to touch down at the posts, and then kick the goal to become the new record holder!

He went on to collect 21 out of the 27 points scored by the Lions in the match and so casual is this modest young man in his approach to big rugby (and it has nothing to do with over-confidence or big headedness), that he arrived at the ground without a proper pair of boots, having two left boots in his bag. A police motor cyclist was enlisted to drive back to the Hotel St George for the famous 'right boot' and John was able to take the field, 'properly shod' with seconds to spare!

To prove his considerable versatility, John produced a try, a dropped goal, three penalties and three conversions to bring his total for the tour to 123 points, and to 115 in New Zealand. These figures were achieved in nine matches to make him the most prolific points scorer in Lions' history. Only one record remained for him to better and that was the individual record of Malcolm Thomas of Wales, who scored 25 points at Nelson in the opening match of the 1950 tour. His 21 points was also behind Hiller's

23 of 1968 in South Africa and Terry Davies' 23 against North Auckland in 1959.

After Barry John's 11 points in the first half, Collins got his first try early in the second before John made one for Duckham which John converted. He then kicked a penalty and dropped a goal before Collins got another splendid try for the Varsities. Finally, the turbulent young Welsh wing, John Bevan raced over for another try in the closing seconds and John converted to leave it at 27–6. The Varsities, through their enterprise and fine spirit, were deserving of several more points.

In his after-match speech at Wellington, Douglas Smith told the assembled company that Mick Hipwell was out of the tour and that a replacement had been asked for from the four Home Unions. This had been rumoured a few days earlier but no actual decision had been taken until lunchtime on Tuesday when Smith had been informed that Hipwell had a torn cartilege which required removing. This followed an examination by three specialists. Thus another test forward had been 'dispatched' by Canterbury – how the Lions loved Canterbury after this – but the injury was started in the N.S.W. match at Sydney early in the tour, and completed at Christchurch.

This brought the total 'wounded' and out-of-action to three, and had the effect of weakening the strength and 'know-how' of the Lions' pack. However, the replacement, Rodger Arneil, should have been originally selected, although he was nominated as a reserve. Tall, strong, and a forager, he was a success in South Africa in 1968, and the Lions were glad to see him when he arrived in Christchurch looking healthy, fit and sun-tanned as he reported to his 1968 colleagues, 'I am very pleased to have made it, and have been keeping fit on a farm!' Immediately, Douglas Smith and Carwyn James, smiled at him and said, 'Rodger, you will play on Wednesday!'

Carwyn James ran the team vigorously on Thursday with two sessions and then allowed them a rest day on Friday, when the team appeared reasonably confident but certainly not overconfident. They were relaxed and ready but not, I feel, prepared for the extremely greasy nature of the ground at Lancaster Park.

On Thursday night the Canterbury Rugby Supporters' Club had a social evening at which Carwyn James and Cliff Morgan were first 'quizzed' about the tour, and then Terry McLean, Terry

O'Connor and myself formed a forum to discuss rugby football in general. This was most enjoyable. O'Connor delivered an oration that was a mixture of Churchill and Bill Ramsay, after he had objected to being called an Englishman by chairman, John Graham! McLean pleaded for more co-operation from the N.Z.R.U., and attempted to point out that up until then the tour had been a great success because British rugby was on the upgrade and not because New Zealand rugby was on the downgrade.

Christchurch had recovered from the Canterbury match and we did not have to contact any officials, other than vice-president Russell Thomas, an excellent press liaison officer, and with Chick McHugh and Harry Innes probably the best of the tour. His plan was help everyone and ensure that they left Christchurch believing it was a friendly city, as indeed it is. Nothing was too much trouble for him, and I can say that the Press Gang were indebted to him for his kindness and readiness to help. Such an official would make an excellent tour manager.

I found the Post Office Telegraph and Telephone Service most efficient and helpful throughout New Zealand. Nothing was too much trouble for them at any time of the day or night, and the fact that you could lift up the phone anywhere and just ask for your home number in Cardiff, and be switched through, immediately, was a great comfort. Again, I could only give a few days notice at Wellington for a 'hot line' to Cardiff to be put into the press seats at Christchurch, and the Wellington office set the ball rolling and the Telephone Manager at Christchurch saw the job finished with an attractive phone near my seat in Lions' scarlet, but this didn't bring the side any special luck!

The United Services Hotel looked after us extremely well and I had an excellent quiet room, although many good friends, visiting from Invercargill and staying on other side of corridor, whooped it up a little on Friday and Saturday nights, as would any other group of rugby supporters! The mid-day buffet lunch proved a change at Christchurch and I always enjoy background music provided by a piano. This allowed Cliff Morgan and myself to burst into song between the consommé and the cold roast beef, and there was always Vivian to enquire whether the chef would risk his hand at making a tasty Welsh rarebit! At every hotel when it came to the sweet course, he would confound the waitresses with the request, 'Could the chef cook me a Welsh rarebit?' The answer was generally, 'The chef regrets he is too busy!... but there came a day, at Masterton, when the menu proudly ended with the world famous savoury and Vivian celebrated!

I had a pleasant evening with Jim Tweedie and his charming family, recently moved to a lovely new house near the Airport at Christchurch, and we talked about many things, vastly removed from rugby football, and it was a pleasant change, but in the main we talked about young people and two of Jim's children, Andrew and Marilyn, gave me much information about normal young folk in New Zealand.

On Friday evening I had a session with a dozen former R.N.V.R. officers at the officer's club in Christchurch and it was good fun, and most impressive was the love of these men for the British Isles. They held responsible jobs in the city, but for all the strange happenings in Europe and the E.E.C., they still put Britain first and this gave me much pleasure, as one had served with these chaps and there was a bond of trust and friendship that could not be broken. I appreciate this everytime I meet Jim Tweedie and shake him by the hand. Call us what you may... our young lives were shaped by six years of war... not that we want our own children similarly involved... for we hope they and their children can be spared such tragedy.

Saturday morning dawned fine and cold; a real winter's morn, and the papers appeared uncertain as to what would happen in the afternoon, while Douglas Smith, with his own special brand of humour, suggested that the New Zealand selectors had still left a 'weak link' in the All Blacks side. This set everyone asking the question 'Who is the weak link?'... and Colin Meads used it to good effect in his dressing room talk telling his men there was to be no weak link! The propaganda war, albeit good natured, was on. The crowds outside the ground and the long queues at the turnstiles started to form at dawn and by the time Vivian, Tudor, Cliff and myself, set off in a scarlet Cortina for the special car park alongside the ground, with our picnic lunches in the boot at just past midday, the popular bank was almost full!

Seventeenth Match
Versus New Zealand (Second Test) at Lancaster Park, Christchurch, July 10.

The Second Test

New Zealand won by two goals (including penalty try), one penalty and three tries (22) to one penalty, one dropped and two tries (12).

Weather: Dry. *Crowd:* 60,000. *Ground:* Muddy and slippery.
Teams:
NEW ZEALAND: L. W. Mains; B. A. Hunter, H. T. Joseph, W. D. Cottrell, B. G. Williams; R. E. Burgess, S. M. Going; B. L. Muller, R. T. Norton, R. A. Guy, R. J. Whiting, C. E. Meads (capt.), I. A. Kirkpatrick, A. J. Wyllie, A. M. McNaughton.
BRITISH ISLES: J. P. R. Williams; T. G. R. Davies, C. M. H. Gibson, S. J. Dawes (capt.), D. J. Duckham; B. John, G. O. Edwards; J. McLauchlan, J. V. Pullin, J. F. Lynch, W. D. Thomas, W. J. McBride, P. J. Dixon, T. M. Davies, J. Taylor.
Referee: Mr J. R. P. Pring (Auckland).

The gates at Lancaster Park were shut, temporarily, at 2 p.m. and then opened again, and it is reported that no spectators were left outside but whether they were able to see clearly remains unsolved. The Canterbury Union and the N.Z.R.U. are now considering whether to make the next test there an 'all ticket' affair and it would appear to be the wisest course of action. If they were to adopt the principle of all-ticket, then they could allow 'live' TV for the second half of each test match in order to meet the demands of the N.Z.B.C. and the great following among the public.

The teams fielded and, as the All Blacks won the toss, the Lions kicked off and soon there was a kick up-field by New Zealand which Williams could not gather. It appeared to be knocked well forward by advancing New Zealand forwards. The ball was kicked dead and a scrum five ordered. The All Blacks won the scrum and almost got over on the blind-side and then forced another scrum which they won again. Going went blind and sent Burgess racing through diagonally over the Lions goal line in the left corner for a clever try, with Mains kicking just wide with his conversion attempt.

First blood to New Zealand, and they looked impressive at this stage with Going controlling affairs at scrum-half. Mains kicked wide with a 45 yard penalty attempt; Burgess was wide with a drop at goal, and it was 20 minutes before the Lions almost scored when Dawes fell upon a dropped pass and Gibson booted through to follow up. New Zealand were forced to kick dead and the Lions pressed for a while before the All Blacks returned to the Lions half of the field and Going put up a high one.

The brave John Williams gathered it and set off to the right, making ground before feeding Dawes, who ran well to hand on to Gibson, and he put Davies away with 40 yards to go. The Welsh wing ran exceedingly well and shook off two would-be tacklers to run round half way out on right. Unfortunately, Barry John was just wide with his conversion attempt of this splendid try and it was three-all, but only for five minutes.

The All Blacks pressed again and Barry John, slipping on the treacherous surface, was forced over in defence for a scrum five. Going went away with his back row and they all surged over the Lions line together with several defenders but Going was awarded a try. Mains converted with a good kick and it was 8–3. The All Blacks were winning plenty of ball, especially from the line-out and ruck, and set up their attacks through their back-row forwards and halves. If the ball was moved further along, however, they were well held by the Lions' outer defences.

Seven minutes from the interval, McNaughton was penalised for getting to Edwards too quickly at a line-out and John kicked a good goal, out of the mud, from 35 yards to make it 8–6. This appeared to give new heart to the Lions although the All Blacks, due to their territorial advantage and greater possession, deserved their interval lead. Yet, one felt that John having missed a penalty and a conversion, had let the All Blacks get away with five points which would have put the Lions in the lead. Normally, he would have done this, only he found himself in difficulty kicking round the corner in the mud, for the left leg tended to move at moment of impact.

The sun came out during the interval and the overcast sky cleared as if to announce that the All Blacks would win because it shone directly into the faces of the Lions! Anyway, Meads had won the toss and so it was the luck of the draw. From the restart the Lions played with greater spirit and searched for the score that would give them the lead. Edwards dropped for goal and the ball sailed low, and in the circumstances it would have been wiser to have let it go, but had he kicked the goal, then it would have been the right course of action!

Then came another near miss when the Lions moved away and

switched their attack to leave Taylor going hard, deep into the All Blacks '25', but either he did not see an unmarked Dixon on his left, or he felt he could get there, for he was tackled short of the line and no score resulted. The All Blacks eventually moved back to attack and just short of ten minutes after the restart the vital incident of the match took place and this proved decisive.

Going went down the wide blind side of a set scrum from 30 yards out and was eventually taken by John Williams short of the Lions' line, as he was in the act of passing. The ball appeared to go forward over the Lions' goal line and, at the same time, Gerald Davies tackled Bryan Williams from behind. They fell over the line together and we thought . . . near thing . . . but Referee Pring spoke to Gerald Davies and then ran to the posts to award New Zealand a penalty try. I feel this came as a surprise to everyone at the time, including probably all the New Zealand side if they were to admit it.

In the opinion of the referee, it would have been a try, even though the ball went forward after the tackle of Going, and while several members of the N.Z.R.U. Council told me that it should have been a penalty kick, the New Zealand press waded in with 'justifiable action', at least almost all except for one, Eric Boggs, former All Black of the Auckland *Eight O'Clock*.

It seemed to me a harsh judgement, but honestly made, and completely turned the course of the match as the Lions fell from 6–8 down to 6–13 and this meant they were seven points and not two behind. It hit them hard, very hard, but lifted the All Blacks up to the clouds and put them in an excellent position. There was no doubt of the fact that Davies did tackle Williams without the ball but would the try have been allowed had he got to the ball that rolled forward over the line?

After 22 minutes the All Blacks went further ahead when Going went to the open side and switched with Burgess who then ran round behind the scrum to the blind side and slipped over as Davies stayed out to mark his man Bryan Williams, and the other Lions failed to 'block the hole'. Mains kicked wide and then Barry John failed with two penalty attempts out of the mud before Mains kicked a goal when McBride had impeded Joseph after he had kicked to the corner. Before this goal the Lions had gone away left with Williams in the line and Duckham had turned back inside to 'score', reasonably near the posts. It could have been five points but Pring blew for a forward pass, again to the surprise of the Lions, as the TV film revealed.

Next came a thrilling try by Kirkpatrick, stealing the ball from a smuggled maul and racing 45 yards to score with several Lions failing to tackle him. It was a fine try by a forward but the Lions, for one of three occasions in the match, were lacking in defence. He should not have been allowed to get there, but get there he did, in the right corner and the crowd erupted! It was all over now at 22–6, since Mains missed the goal, with only five minutes to go, but the Lions attacked gaily and effectively. John Williams joined the line again, moving right, and Gerald Davies was given a run from the '25', his speed taking him outside Mains for a lovely try in the corner. John could not convert it but before the final whistle, he dropped a lovely goal from 30 yards, and it was all over at 22–12.

New Zealand were level in the series, and deservedly so, but it had not been the 'Day of the Lions' for they had missed their chances while the All Blacks had taken theirs, and they had not enjoyed the rub of the green at Dunedin. There was disappointment at first, naturally, for Carwyn James thought the chances had been there 'for the taking' and that victory could have been gained. Nevertheless he paid tribute to the All Blacks forwards although neither he, nor Douglas Smith and John Dawes, made any mention of the penalty try in their speeches at the after-match function.

Meads cleverly referred to the 'weak link' in the New Zealand side and hoped that the selectors would pick him again! All agreed it was a fine game of rugby football at test match level while James said he had no complaint against referee Pring who 'Had taken charge of two fine test matches'. One sensed then that he would ask for him again for the Third Test, if he were put on the panel of four. It was an exciting and hard test, causing even Meads to say it was one of the hardest he had played in, but there were questions to be asked on both sides, following an evening of celebration by both sides at the United Services Hotel.

The New Zealand press, and who can blame them, gave the All Blacks deserved praise for their effort. The TV tried to discuss the penalty try by stopping the film during a discussion on Monday, after the film had been shown on Sunday evening when Lions watched it at Masterton on arrival from Christchurch. The film did not reveal much but Terry McLean, Gabe David, Lindsay

Knight and Earle Read, the travelling 'mob', came down in favour of it and heavily!

One thing I could never understand after this match was the fact that not one New Zealand paper, on Monday, quoted what the British Sunday papers had to say about the match or any paper quote what Monday morning UK papers said about it. This was most strange for so much was reprinted after the Canterbury match and first test.

On Sunday morning I listed the strength and weaknesses of the Lions test team, as I had seen them at Christchurch, and then drew some conclusions which I sent to the Thomson Morning papers. First the Lions had unusual pace and ability in attack behind the scrum; they had cleverer backs even allowing for Going's fine match at scrum-half and the improvement of Burgess; and the Lions had the ability to counter attack and a remarkable young rugby hero in full-back, John Williams.

Among their weaknesses were the following: Indecisive close to scrum cover defence; lack of line-out support for jumper and failure to block opponents charging through on to tapped down ball; lack of overall speed to rucks; Duckham not quite as forceful as Bevan on left-wing and Barry John not as accurate as normally, while place kicking out of mud.

Suggestions for improvement... need to bring more vigorous Bevan back to left-wing position; need to get Edwards really match fit and confident in himself that his hamstring would stand up to 80 minutes; bigger back-row required with Arneil to play regularly and be included in third test, and also Quinnell included if fit to make tall trio of Arneil, Quinnell and Davies. Finally, to improve line-out jumping and make it more specialised by a study of New Zealand blocking methods while, at the same time, hope for dry ground, so that backs would be able to run freely and not be bogged down on a slippery surface.

Full marks to Colin Meads and his team for taking advantage of the situation to bring New Zealand level in series, but now the time had come for the Lions to rebuild and concentrate, as they had done earlier in the tour.

On Sunday morning it was good to have Charles Saxton come in and talk to us before we set off for Wellington where we were entertained by the local journalists, who were extremely pleasant and kind, and showed that throughout the world, at heart, most journalists are alike, if some be more constructive in their criticism than others. In rugby football it is possible to divide them into two groups; those who love the game more dearly than sensation, and *vice versa*, but the Lions tour, because of its pleasant nature, and the diplomacy of management and players, was making it hard for the sensation men at this stage!

Later came a pleasant drive by rental cars 'over the hill' to Masterton and the comfortable and helpful Empire Hotel. The young waitresses were the quickest things on two legs seen in any dining hall in New Zealand.

Masterton, which is a lovely country town of nearly 20,000 people, is the centre of the Wairarapa, the home of two famous All Blacks at number eight, Atholl 'Tonk' Mahoney of 1935 fame and Brian Lochore of 1967, two outstanding sportsmen and gentlemen, who have done much to prove that big men in New Zealand can be gentlemen, on and off the field. They have happy faces and big hands when you greet them and they are both proud and grateful for the privilege of visiting the U.K.

The Lions had a wonderful day shooting, fishing, golfing and eating, with members of the East Coast Club at Castle Point, a favourite summer watering place in the Wairarapa, but work kept the Welsh members of the press party at the hotel. This is one of the hazards of touring, for the typewriter is always beckoning and demanding! Rain continued to fall throughout our stay and continued even on Wednesday morning, suggesting that the Lions would be ankle-deep in mud in the afternoon, battling against a terrier-like Wairarapa-Bush side.

Eighteenth Match
Versus Wairarapa-Bush at Memorial Park, Masterton, July 14. Lions won by three goals and four tries (27) to one dropped and one penalty (6).
Weather: Showery. *Ground:* Muddy. *Crowd:* 10,000.
Teams:
WAIRARAPA-BUSH: V. D. Marfell; K. E. O'Shea, B. G. Martin, N. A. Purvis, M. Barnes; R. T. Couch, L. H. Karatau (capt.); W. N. Rowlands, G. E. Falconer, W. J. Crawley, D. P. Oliver, B. J. Lochore, P. J. Ryan, R. R. Brock, G. N. Gray.
BRITISH ISLES: R. B. Hiller (capt.); J. S. Spencer, A. J. Lewis, C. W. W. Rea, A. G. Biggar; B. John, G. O. Edwards; C. B. Stevens, F. A. L. Laidlaw, M. G. Roberts, G. L. Brown, T. G.

Evans, R. J. Arneil, D. L. Quinnell, J. F. Slattery.
Referee: Mr R. D. Macey (Nelson-Bays).

Conditions promised a very poor match for it had rained for weeks in Masterton, and Memorial Park had received little or no chance to dry out. Even on the morning of the match it showered heavily and, as the large crowd of enthusiasts filled the stand and enclosure, it was raining. Such conditions were said to favour the local side, reinforced for the match by Brian Lochore, who had retired from big football but was ready to help in an emergency.

Yet it proved to be a most enjoyable match with Wairarapa-Bush dominating the first half with their lively forward work and the Lions taking charge in the second, through accurate running and handling in the mud. It was a most encouraging effort on the part of the Lions, whose forwards improved as the game progressed, and whose backs enjoyed running and handling. The playing of a big back-row of Arneil, Quinnell and Slattery revealed the necessity for such men at the end of the line-out in New Zealand, but John Taylor was to play superbly in the Third and Fourth Tests to upset this theory!

At first the Combined forwards burst through the line-out and round the ends to prey upon Edwards and it was difficult for the scrum-half, putting him under the same pressure as he was in the Second Test match. Then the Lions improved and closed the gaps and Brown and Evans worked well together to get better ball which eased the pressure on Edwards, and in turn he was able to send his flowing service to John, whose accurate handling did not suffer in the mud. However, the combined spoilers were harassing and Wairarapa-Bush took the lead in the 25th minute with a penalty goal by Marfell from 28 yards, after the Lions were adjudged inside ten yards at a line-out. As this law was not often employed in New Zealand it led to increased pressure on the Lions halves at the line-out.

They maintained their pressure for quite 35 minutes like busy terriers about the field, yet always clean and sporting. The crowd encouraged them and one had to admire their persistence; especially that of flank-forward Gray and scrum-half Karatau, who led the side. However, before the interval, the Lions first equalised and then took the lead and it was the 'razzle-dazzle' of Barry John that did it. He moved away from a set scrum to the blind side and wriggled through for a try that Hiller could not convert. Then, getting the ball from a line-out, the Lions moved left and Biggar crashed over the line, on the far wing, as he was tackled.

John failed with the conversion but the scene was set for a full Lions' recovery in the second half and they went well. After 11 minutes John appeared to score, after Rea had knocked-on outside the line, but the try was awarded and John converted it. Next came a splendid try from Spencer, who had his best match of the tour, but John was wide with the conversion. Edwards touched down for a try that John converted after the Combined side had failed to clear their line. Biggar got another good one, followed by one from John, his third of the match, after clever interpassing with Lewis. Hiller converted this beautifully from the touch-line and then, in the closing minutes, Couch scored a try for the Combined side that was well deserved, and the match ended at 27–6.

Criticism of the Lions in the Masterton match was mixed but players and management were encouraged by the second half form of the team and, especially, the forwards. Arneil's form was most impressive for a first match, while Quinnell made a welcome return to the side and form. Poor Chris Rea tried desperately hard and used his considerable speed but was completely out of luck, although he should have been awarded a try as a result of following up a kick-ahead by Barry John, whereas the controversial try awarded to Barry John should not have been allowed.

The evening was a pleasant one and the staff of the Empire Hotel created a new 'speed record' for service at dinner and the tradition of taking a 'sip of the wine' after a victory was observed. The next morning we set off for Napier, having wished Terry McLean a happy birthday, only to find on arrival at Tonk Mahoney's in Konini, that it was also *his* birthday. His wife had 'baked a cake' but, in deference to his youthful enthusiasm for living, she placed only one candle on it. It was a most enjoyable lunch and 'Morgan the Organ' played delightfully on the piano while the Welsh 'mafia' sang traditional songs for the occasion.

It was a couple of hours of relaxation, so necessary on tour from time to time, and really the best way of getting to know New Zealanders, for one cannot judge or know the heart of a country from an hotel room. One has to go out among the people and into their homes. For this reason, though I first met him in 1935, I got to know Tonk Mahoney a lot better, as I have so many of the 1935 and 1945 teams, and perhaps much of this is due to the fact that they are of my own generation, disturbed by World War II, or should I say, matured by its experiences, both good and bad.

The rain fell hard from Konini to Napier and on arrival there the breakers that pounded the long and pleasant beach, were bigger and noiser than those seen on any previous visit. Yet Napier had many pleasant memories for me (Gwen was with me in 1966) and, as at Gisborne and other places visited, local officials and friends were most kind to us.

The Press Gang were splendidly entertained at Napier on two evenings at the Hawkes Bay Club, once by the local press and once by the local Union, and the gatherings were pleasant with photographer Peter Bush in most amusing form on Friday evening after a visit to the local wine-growers with some of the Lions party. The President of the N.Z.R.U. was a Hawkes Bay man, Mr Bramwell, who was kindly and sociable, as were other officials.

It had rained hard, on and off, for several weeks in Hawkes Bay, during a mild winter, and this had left McLean Park extremely heavy. However, a call at Alex McDonald's pleasant home enabled us to inspect the residential area of the city. The lawns and flowers were exceedingly healthy, as one would expect from a seaside resort in a pleasant climate. Again, Saturday dawned dry and clear and promised better conditions than anticipated earlier in the week but, on arrival at McLean Park one found, quite naturally, that it was greasy on the surface.

Nineteenth Match
Versus Hawkes Bay at McLean Park, Napier, July 17, 1971.
Lions won by two goals, two penalties, one dropped goal and two tries (25) to one dropped goal and one penalty (6).
Weather: Showery. *Ground:* Greasy. *Crowd:* 24,500
Teams:
HAWKES BAY: I. R. Bishop; R. Hunter, M. G. Duncan, I. R. McRae, D. G. Curtis; B. D. M. Furlong (capt.), H. J. Paewai; H. Meech, B. E. McLeod, N. W. Thimbleby, G. T. Wiig, K. K. Crawford, G. A. Condon, J. J. Wilson and T. Thornton.
BRITISH ISLES: J. P. R. Williams; T. G. R. Davies, C. M. H.

Gibson, S. J. Dawes, J. C. Bevan; B. John, G. O. Edwards; J. McLauchlan, J. V. Pullin, M. G. Roberts, G. L. Brown, G. J. Evans, R. J. Arneil, T. M. Davies, J. F. Slattery.
Referee: Mr R. J. Watson (North Auckland).

Although the Lions won this match comfortably, through the speed and accuracy of their back play, it was not a match they enjoyed playing in and they told me they rated it next to Canterbury, as the most disagreeable up to that time. Fortunately, it was marked by some magnificent running by Gerald Davies who proved himself one of the great wings of the day by scoring four superb tries. There was a 'flare-up' in the final minutes during which the Welsh half-backs revealed their complete disgust for the nature of the rugby played by the opposition.

The reception they received from the crowd, was naturally abusive, while the press box appeared to be divided. Pat Marshall gave them a 'grilling' in the *Sunday Express* which was not particularly well received, as one can imagine, in Wales. However, they had just about had enough of it and could stand no more by the time the final whistle approached, and they showed their disgust. John had spent much of the afternoon avoiding late tackles and scoring points, to the obvious disgust of the Hawkes Bay coach sitting behind the British press in the stand. In the end John caught the ball and waited in his own '25' while the opposition came up to him before kicking. This was taken as an intended taunt to both the Hawkes Bay players and the crowd, while Edwards after being caught in a maul by his hair and 'given the knee', appeared to let fly at a Hawkes Bay man on the ground. The crowd roared its disapproval and, perhaps, great players should not have allowed their feelings to show. However, there comes a time when even the greatest cannot stand any more, and this was one such occasion.

After 30 minutes play in the first half, John Pullin had to be assisted from the field as a result of a punch in the eye delivered by a 'friendly' Hawkes Bay forward. The eye was badly cut and, unfortunately for Hawkes Bay, the substitution law saw to it that the Lions did not lose by the blow. The play had a touch of Canterbury about it, and since both provincial sides had forwards who were a little past their best, it made one think!

On the brighter side, Gerald Davies had a superb afternoon,

and his four tries scored after 12, 13, and 43 minutes of the first half and 40 minutes of the second half were as fine a group as I have ever seen scored by a Lions' wing or, indeed, any other wing. He simply sparkled and employed all his skills with the jink, side-step, swerve and sudden burst of acceleration. Carwyn James thought his last try, scored when in the centre after Gibson had left the field with a hamstring, was the best, for he suddenly shot through during a passing movement, leaving his colleagues and opponents behind as if they were stationary. One felt he was saying 'I am a good wing but what do you think of me as a centre?', yet, as a modest, pleasant young man, nothing was further from his mind.

I thought his third try, just before the interval, his best, although all four were of a special quality and revealed the paucity of the play of Hawkes Bay behind the scrum. They lacked pace and imagination throughout, even though they had two All Blacks, Furlong and MacRae at five eighth. When Davies jinked through two converging defenders, like a man dodging the guillotine, the difference in class was most marked. They fell to the ground alongside each other as Davies finished at the posts!

Hawkes Bay started well enough, rattling the Lions before they had settled down and taking the lead after seven minutes with a snap dropped goal, well taken by flank-forward Thornton, when the Lions were under pressure. Then Bishop had a drop at goal from full-back but the ball rebounded into the arms of John Williams, who started an attack that ended in Davies scoring his first try between the posts. John converted easily and instead of being 6–0 in the lead Hawkes Bay trailed by 5–3. It was the turning point in the match as Hawkes Bay decided then to close the play down and adopt a defensive approach which availed them nothing except to produce a niggling match when they could well have enjoyed themselves more. There is a lesson in this... spend your time attacking, if you can, because there are many occasions when you cannot, and just have to defend!

Two Welshmen scored all the points for the Lions – Davies with four tries and John with two penalties, two conversions and a dropped goal. For Hawkes Bay, Thornton dropped a goal and Bishop kicked a penalty. The speeches after the match were interesting, with Dawes drawing attention to the spirit of the game. New Zealand speakers said the 'closing minutes' were part of the game – perhaps in some parts of New Zealand, one would think this, but not at the majority of centres.

During the night there was a little 'horse play' in one of the corridors, while several of the Lions relaxed on Sunday morning at the Tom and Jim Lowry farms. Tom provided drinks and Jim an excellent cold lunch with good company including members of his family. It was great fun and there was singing round the piano followed by an amusing car trip to Napier Airport with the aid of a 'pathfinder'. We 'made' the plane and arrived at Gisborne Airport to be met by a most efficient and friendly press liaison officer, Chick McHugh, and my old naval friend Don Grant and his daughter who conveyed me to the Sandowne Motel, where we found there was no 'room at the inn'. Although every other member of the party was accommodated, Jenkins, Morgan and Thomas were excluded. For the first time in three trips to New Zealand, the traditional hospitality had fallen down.

It was a real 'upco' as Hiller would say and, of course, no one was said to be responsible, as each group blamed the other! It was, to say the least, bad organisation, and considering I had written to the hotel, confirming my room, months before the tour started, it was a right poor show! However, Chick McHugh whisked us away to the Orange Grove Motel, where the three of us spent four happy days as the 'mafia in exile' planning further 'manoeuvres' with, I am glad to say, the help of the friendly Poverty Bay Rugby Union. In emergency, one must always have friends!

CHAPTER EIGHT

The Third Test

On the two previous visits to Gisborne I had watched the Lions play under severe pressure and only just succeed against the enthusiastic combined Poverty Bay and East Coast sides. In 1959 Terry Davies was truly magnificent at full-back in dealing with the up and unders, and Andrew Mulligan extremely brave in appearing in the match on the Wednesday, after joining the party straight from Britain only two days previously! In 1966 it was a struggle, with Gibson's try bringing happy relief and a 9–6 win, but I remember best that my wife had joined me on the Sunday and it was her first Lions match. She sat near the press box and at half time put her head to the window and said, 'Give me my air ticket, as I will not be able to stand much more of this!'

Yet how much would she have enjoyed the 1971 tour with its continuous run of magnificent success, and yet another hard match at Gisborne. One thing that does not change, with the passing of the years, is the oustanding hospitality of the city of Gisborne and its people. So many officials and friends asked after my wife, and of players of previous tours, and my ex-naval friend Don Grant was there with his family to entertain me. Chick McHugh and the Gisborne Club members were nice people and, despite the rain and the threat of a heavy ground, one knew there would be a full house at the ground and perhaps a record crowd.

Cliff Morgan proved himself an expert cooker of breakfast at the Orange Grove Motel and we drank gallons of instant coffee and considerably less of the 'hard stuff'. Carwyn James and Barry John called for afternoon tea, with Vivian presiding and Cliff brewing, while Tonk Mahoney and his family called with half of his son's rugby team to see us on the morning of the match; his son played in the curtain raiser. We gave Tonk a 'pot' for his birthday on behalf of the Welsh 'mafia' and he was especially pleased. We had happy days shopping and these are the small things one remembers of a tour.

Twentieth Match
Versus Poverty Bay and East Coast at Rugby Park, Gisborne, July 21.
Lions won by two dropped goals, one penalty and three tries (18) to three penalties and one try (12).
Weather: Sunny. *Ground:* Very Muddy. *Crowd:* 15,000 (record).
Teams:
COMBINED XV: W. K. Mabey; P. S. Ransley, R. M. Parkinson, G. R. Newlands, A. J. Cross; P. A. Martin, P. J. Duncan; R. J. Ussher, G. Allen, D. Walker, K. Allen, K. G. McGrannachan, D. A. Kirkpatrick, D. T. W. Repa, I. A. Kirkpatrick (capt).
BRITISH ISLES: R. B. Hiller; D. J. Duckham, A. J. Lewis, S. J. Dawes (capt), A. G. Biggar; C. W. W. Rea, G. O. Edwards; C. B. Stevens, F. A. L. Laidlaw, J. F. Lynch, W. D. Thomas, G. J. Evans, D. Quinnell, P. J. Dixon, J. Taylor.
Referee: Mr R. E. Courtney (Auckland).

Yet again the Combined side rose magnificently to the occasion and gave the Lions a really hard time of it. Although the Tourists deserved to win in the end, it was quite a close call. They did not take the chances that would have provided them with a more comfortable win and it was 15–12 in their favour with only seconds left for play when Dawes dropped a special goal from 40 yards to really clinch the issue. There were seven test men in the Lions side and so they were strong enough, but the fire of the Combined forwards had to be matched and in this Derek Quinnell played extremely well to suggest that his knee was now right, and that he could be played in the Third Test and look after the younger Kirkpatrick.

Laidlaw, Dixon and Evans also went well but although Edwards was a hard worker at scrum half the rest of the backs did not function smoothly enough. Chris Rea was not really happy at outside-half but John and Gibson had to be rested and had Hopkins been fit he would have played at scrum-half. Duckham ran well on the wing but Hiller was matched as a place kicker by the rival full-back, Mabey, who landed three good goals.

The Third Test

However, there was some dispute over the Combined try scored from a quick throw-in from touch, which prop forward Ussher collected and dived over to score. At the after-match function, John Dawes raised the point, and it was the first occasion on the tour for any Lions' spokesman to question a referee's decision. Dawes pointed out that Item Five of Section B of Law 23, governing a quick throw-in, was not being observed in New Zealand, since for a quick throw-in, the ball must be handled only by the player concerned and not by the crowd or ball boys. This comment made the headlines as did that by Doug Smith that curtain raisers should not be played on wet and muddy grounds – to which New Zealand officials replied that it opened up the ground and allowed air to get at it, as well as aiding drainage. At Masterton and Gisborne the grounds were both heavy but they appeared to dry a little during the match.

One felt at this stage that the strain of a long and successful tour was starting to tell on the Lions and they were waiting to acquire their second wind. It was good to see Laidlaw back in form and McLauchlan doing his stuff at prop, while Evans did his work as a tight forward. Quinnell kept Ian Kirkpatrick reasonably quiet and at the end of the match the All Black went to hospital for treatment for a recurring rib muscle injury. He was worried about his Third Test place but medical examination revealed that he would be able to play.

The Combined pack went really well and Duncan was a lively scrum-half with Martin and Newlands opportunist at five-eighths, while Mabey at full-back had a splendid day. There appeared to be confusion concerning some of the referee's decisions, from both sides, and I was amused by John Dawes' comment after the match that the referee would be remembered for his efforts. However, the Lions were full of praise for the Combined team's fine showing and stood in two lines to clap them off the field, which was a sincere gesture, well-deserved by a side possessing splendid spirit and one that upheld the fine traditions of previous matches.

We had an enjoyable evening in the Chalets and the next day flew into Auckland and set up again at the Royal International Hotel which, on reflection, was our happiest 'place of rest'. All the staff looked after us excedingly well and there were a few 'special' ones like Gwenyth and Bridie who saw to it that the

Press Gang was comfortably housed on the sixth floor, away from the madding crowd. Again, in Auckland, there were some delightful and sophisticated eating places like 'La Boheme' and 'Top of the Town' and one tasted their delights. 'La Boheme' had much to offer while the view from the 'Top of the Town' was most romantic.

Auckland was the twenty-first match of the tour, and they were known to be a good side and had worked hard in their preparations, studying the Lions closely, even with films, as late as the Thursday evening before the match. They included five All Blacks in their side and their captain, Cullimore, had played for three years with the London Scottish. More interesting still, for the Lions, was the inclusion at first five eighth of Peter Murdoch. He was an All Black and son of Doc Murdoch, the official Lions masseur and himself a former Auckland player. Peter had the task of attempting to match Barry John and there was a great deal of leg pull for Doc, inwardly as anxious as any father would be for his son on the day before the big match.

At this stage of the tour the B.B.C. jumped into real action; indeed they stepped up their efforts for rugby football almost to the standard of World Cup football, and Cliff Morgan was able to tell me that through use of satellite Intelstar the Third Test would be shown on 'Grandstand' and that possibly the Fourth Test 'live' at 3.30 a.m. in the British Isles. Although this did not prove possible, the Fourth Test was also shown on 'Grandstand' on the Saturday afternoon.

Twenty-First Match
Versus Auckland at Eden Park, Auckland, July 24.
Lions won by two goals and three penalties (19) to three penalties and one dropped goal (12).
Weather: Sunny and warm. *Ground:* Firm. *Crowd:* 55,000
Teams:
AUCKLAND: R. G. Whatman; B. G. Williams, K. R. Carrington, G. E. Weinberg, D. L. Palmer; P. H. Murdoch, D. M. McIntyre; G. D. Denholm, R. A. Urlich, B. R. Johnstone, J. Sherlock, P. J. Whiting, B. A. Edwards, J. P. Posa, N. R. Cullimore (capt).
BRITISH ISLES: J. P. R. Williams; T. G. R. Davies, J. S. Spencer, S. J. Dawes (capt), D. J. Duckham; B. John, G. O. Edwards; J. McLauchlan, J. V. Pullin, M. G. Roberts, G. J.

Evans, G. L. Brown, R. J. Arneil, T. M. Davies J. F. Slattery. *Referee:* Mr. W. L. Adlam (Wanganui).

The Lions had nine test players in their side and were experimenting again with Mike Roberts as a prop, while Brown and Arneil were getting their chance to prove themselves. The All Blacks selectors were represented as they were to meet to pick their team after this match, before the Lions headed for a short rest 'cure' to the Bay of Islands on the Sunday where they said they would annouce their test side on the Tuesday. Also after the match the Lions would recive their panel of four referees from which to select the official for the Third Test, and I recall saying to John Pring when I walked up the steps of the stand to the Press Box, 'You'll get the job, John, if your name is on the panel!'

It was a beautifully sunny day in Auckland and through the 'aid' of Gwenyth in the Reception Office at the Royal International, we travelled to the ground 'armed' with a magnificent picnic lunch. Sue, Vivian, Cliff, Tudor and myself had much more than an 'adequate sufficiency' and, as my wife has always insisted that I have a good meal before a match, this was in keeping with instructions! The real reason is that you keep healthier through not missing meals, and also enjoy the rugby much more. The Eden Park surface was in excellent condition and fifty-five thousand spectators greeted the teams when they fielded, but no national anthem was played.

It proved to be an exciting match, one of the most exciting of the tour outside the tests, and Auckland went perilously near to winning, causing even the placid John Dawes to remark. 'I was not really worried but a little concerned!' In the Press Box the atmosphere was a little tense at times although, after such a run of success and with such confidence in the Lions, one really felt that they would not lose. Their ability to come back and run their way out of trouble, and Barry John's expertise as a kicker caused one to have confidence, but in this match, Auckland, according to those who watched them regularly, really played above themselves and on the day earned the title of being the best provincial side met by the Lions up to that time.

They had a superbly drilled pack of forwards, extremely well led by Cullimore, and it was the best scrummaging of the tour against the Lions (the best rucking was Otago's) and through this good scrummaging and speed to the ball with fiery drive, plus kicking on by the two halves, the Lions were often on the defensive. Their goal-line experienced many hair-raising escapes, and for once on tour Barry John did not produce his tactical flair for reading a situation, often kicking when he should have passed, and *vice versa*. Fortunately, Gareth Edwards produced one of his special matches, playing with supreme strength and confidence, and Dawes was immensely steady. One sensed that the back division missed Gibson and also that Gerald Davies would have done better, as he admitted afterwards, had he been a little selfish and tried more on his own!

However, John Williams was in good form at full-back and Barry John's points-scoring right boot was as active as ever – he collected three penalties and two conversions of the tries by Evans and Dawes. Gareth Edwards made both the tries, for he broke wide from a line-out to send Evans diving over, and wide from a scrum to send Dawes over on the inside, near to the Auckland line. They were both vintage Edwards, and all this was most comforting with the Third Test just a week away!

Roberts was not happy in the Lions' front row as tight head and, obviously, there was need to recall Lynch, while Brown did enough to suggest that he would just get in ahead of Delme Thomas. Again, neither wing forward had done more than Quinnell at Gisborne and so the selectors had a few problems left over for for the Tuesday meeting. McBride's shoulder was improving and all hoped that he would make it, although Evans was waiting in the 'wings' for a call, and he did well against Auckland.

John kicked a penalty to put the Lions in the lead and Whatman equalised immediately afterwards. Then John kicked another penalty before he got his try which he converted to make it 11–3 at the interval. John kicked another penalty early in the second half, and one thought that from 14–3 the Lions would race away. Instead, Auckland came back magnificently, full of fire and brimstone with a 55 yard penalty by Bryan Williams and a dropped goal by Murdoch, followed by another Whatman penalty to make it 14–12.

There remained, with stoppages, 20 minutes before the final whistle, but the Lions survived in their traditional manner, and in the final stages they returned to the attack and finished strongly. They won a five yard scrum in the left corner and Edwards ran wide to the open and fed Dawes running straight between Edwards and the scrum. He got over the line, some 18 inches, but was covered with bodies. Referee Adlam was on the spot but a section of the crowd did not agree with his decision to allow the try and some threw empty soft drink cans – there was no beer owing to a brewery strike – onto the in-goal area. It was a try; John kicked the goal and the game was all over at 19–12, a final score that was little hard on Auckland, but indicated quite clearly how difficult it was becoming to beat the Lions.

The press had been allowed into the after-match function on the understanding that they would not report proceedings, but they were allowed to report the New Zealand team for the Third Test, announced in the Club rooms. To the surprise of all, and especially Tom Pearce, the rugged Keith Murdoch of Otago was recalled.

It was not a popular choice among the officials in the Club room and they did not spare the selectors their criticism. When, on Sunday, it was announced that Murdoch had again withdrawn, it came as no surprise. He had become a selectorial 'yo-yo' but this time he had hurt his ribs playing in Club football in Dunedin, so once again the 'prop that never was', as far as the Lions were concerned, was still behind the stage curtain and despite encouragement from selectors would not appear.

On Sunday the Lions moved off to Waitangi, in the Bay of Islands; it was then announced that John Pring would have charge of the Third Test at Wellington, and this was a popular decision for he had matured as a referee since his first test of 1966 at Dunedin, when Meads 'ran the show'. The All Blacks brought back Guy for Murdoch at prop but had to make a further change since Bryan Williams, worried by a groin injury, withdrew and his provincial centre, Carrington, who played in the First Test, took his place. In the Lions camp we felt that Carrington should have been chosen instead of Joseph at centre with Collins of Otago on the wing, if Williams was unfit.

Unfortunately, the Lions had bad weather in the Bay of Islands and as I had remained at Auckland, Tudor rang through at 7.45 on Tuesday morning with the Lions' test side. Duckham had retained his place against the challenge of Bevan, and Quinnell and Slattery had won the flank positions. For the rest it was as predicted, expected and indeed, deserved. After three pleasant and restful days in Auckland, getting up to date, visiting the pictures, and enjoying a harbour cruise, one found Wellington, on arrival there on Thursday afternoon, intensely enthusiastic about the Test.

The team trained before making their hotel and the practice went well except that Slattery was absent with tonsillitis and Taylor stood in for him. Poor Slattery tried hard to recover in time but he failed and while Whiting was forced to withdraw from the All Blacks side, Slattery had to do likewise from the Lions. To the surprise of all, the New Zealand selectors called back Brian Lochore, and 'split the country', while the Lions played for safety and brought in John Taylor.

All this furious selectorial activity ensured that one had enough to write about and the 'trot' to the cable office was a source of exercise, and a way of dodging the hundreds of cheerful visitors who wanted to 'play up' a little, in the lively Hotel St George! On the eve of the match Sue, Vivian and myself were the guests of the 1935 All Blacks and this was both a privilege and a pleasure, for the side was very much in my mind, having watched it against Wales in the magnificent and memorable match of 1935 at the Cardiff Arms Park. Cliff Jones, just arrived from London with a happy party of Lions supporters, had stepped on to New Zealand soil just an hour before he was whisked away to the reunion, and he enjoyed every minute of it.

The weather had been 'playing up' at Wellington all week but Saturday dawned sunny and dry with a strong breeze, not to be classed as a wind in windy Wellington.

Between them, they did wonders for the turf, and there was a considerable improvement by the time we arrived at the ground for our picnic lunch in the car park opposite the grandstand. The lunch was not as good as that at Auckland, for it missed the 'touch of a woman's hand' but, of all picnic lunches Vivian and myself have eaten outside test match grounds, this was the most anxious!

Twenty-Second Match
Versus New Zealand (Third Test) at Athletic Park, Wellington, July 31.

The Third Test

British Isles won by two goals and a dropped goal (13) to a try (3).
Weather: Sunny and windy. *Ground:* Soft and drying. *Crowd:* 50,000.
Teams:
NEW ZEALAND: L. W. Mains; B. A. Hunter, H. J. Joseph, W. D. Cottrell, K. R. Carrington; R. E. Burgess, S. M. Going; B. L. Muller, R. T. Norton, R. Guy, B. J. Lochore, C. E. Meads (capt), I. A. Kirkpatrick, A. J. Wyllie, A. M. McNaughton.
BRITISH ISLES: J. P. R. Williams; T. G. R. Davies, S. J. Dawes (capt), C. M. H. Gibson, D. J. Duckham; B. John, G. O. Edwards; J. McLauchlan, J. V. Pullin, J. F. Lynch, G. L. Brown, W. J. McBride, D. L. Quinnell, T. M. Davies, J. Taylor.
Referee: Mr J. P. Pring (Auckland).

All hail, the 1971 Lions, for in this match they achieved what was once thought to be well nigh impossible – the sharing of a test series in New Zealand. The feat had not been accomplished on a long tour since 1937, when the Springboks had won the series 2-1; now the 1971 Lions, with a magnificent display, had gone one up with one to play, an extremely healthy and happy position. It made millions of followers at home happy; it pleased quite a number of New Zealanders while it sent the Lions team and its camp followers into a mood of ecstasy. For one follower of many years, who had suffered seriously since 1955 in the cause of Lions rugby, it brought immense satisfaction, as pride bubbled to the surface and almost choked the calmest of critics.

I lifted up the 'hot line' to Cardiff, as it rang immediately the match ended, and set off dictating one of the happiest rugby stories it has been my pleasure to record. It may not have been written well but its message was sincere, and the Compact Cable line, made copy taker Bill Hook sound as if he was in a room downstairs. One could not jump up in one's seat, or sing, or drink, or laugh with one's friends. It was a case of gathering one's thoughts, instantaneously, and describing the historic events between 2.30 p.m. and 4.03 p.m. on Saturday afternoon, July 13, 1971 at Athletic Park in Wellington, the capital of New Zealand, a mighty rugby nation!

Yet one was intensely humble at that moment, for it was the

end of a great era for New Zealand in the game and, possibly, the start of a good one for the British Isles as the 'staff' had changed hands. Having suffered defeat with so many Lions' sides with its accompanying sorrow and disappointment, one felt sorry now for New Zealand, but only up to a point, for the victory had been thoroughly deserved and nobly gained. That is where pride entered the mind and sent words of praise flowing into the 'phone and across the seas 13,000 miles away. Douglas Smith and Carwyn James, John Dawes and his players; they were the heroes of this enjoyable and spirited battle that must have warmed the heart of every British rugby follower when its result was known.

It was a considerable achievement for any side to twice defeat New Zealand in a test series on its own soil but it was a major effort for a Lions side and, as a tactical exercise, it revealed how much thought, energy, study and preparation had gone into it. The Lions had been remarkably successful up to this match and their only defeat in New Zealand, before this Third Test, had been in the Second Test, but that match had taught them more about themselves and their opponents than any other, because rather than engage in sorrow and self-pity they looked at themselves and said, 'We can win the Third, since it was our own shortcomings that really lost the Second!' It was positive thinking, and Coach James and Captain Dawes set about preparing their side for victory.

As explained in an earlier chapter, it was the All Blacks' loose forwards; the thrusting of Going at scrum-half, the play at the end of the line-out and the weakness of the near-scrum and near-ruck cover, that lost the Second Test. All this had to be remedied, and it was, some by changes at forward, and some by alteration in method and approach and, above all else, the need to believe that the match could be won.

The back row had to stop Going thrusting to either side of scrum and ruck, and the Lions trio rose nobly to the occasion, for Quinnell, in his first test – and that as an uncapped player – Mervyn Davies and Taylor were superb as a unit, and while Davies continued to grow in stature as the tour progressed, Taylor played the match of his career to extract all the revenge for the sadness of 1969 with Wales.

McBride a true hero of rugby in 1971 led with tremendous enthusiasm and had his men with him, and not behind him as at

Christchurch. The front row stood firm and McLauchlan and Lynch proved once again that they were not 'seconds' but 'firsts'. Brown made a notable début and commanded the line-out for the first vital 25 minutes, while Pullin won two important tight heads when they were needed. Behind these eight, tireless, intelligent, persistent forwards, was the man of the match, Gareth Edwards, proving to New Zealanders, at long last, that he possessed skill, speed, courage and greatness!

With his forwards doing well and the 'holes' in the line-out 'plugged'; with Going held in a vice-like grip; and with possession in his hands, he spun away a series of delightful passes to enable his backs to play magnificently for twenty minutes and build up a lead of 13 points. It was almost incredible; the sight of the Lions backs running and handling, and dazzling a New Zealand defence that was almost swept off its feet by the red and white tidal wave!

Then at two vital moments, Edwards moved away on his own. First to the blind side, to set up Gerald Davies for a try and then to the open side, powerfully, across the defence to put Barry John in for a try. Great moments, and decisive moments in the game which saw a great player prove himself on the hardest 'battlefield' of all: a New Zealand test ground.

Barry John, at outside-half, was also at his immaculate best for he was superbly calm and in control and collected ten of his side's thirteen points with a try, a dropped goal and two conversions. What more could one ask? Gerald Davies on the right wing, running with the speed of the wind and the elusiveness of a scurrying rabbit; Gibson with his long runs and brilliant counters; Dawes with his sure hands and surprising pace; Duckham with his long stride and Williams standing up to it all at full-back despite a kick in the back early on.

The 13 points were scored in 18 minutes before the All Blacks recovered their poise. The golden points 'rush' was started after three minutes when Davies made a glorious run down the touch-line and kicked on. Hunter gathered and was tackled by Taylor for Quinnell to win the ball at the ruck and send it back to Gibson who thought about dropping a goal himself but saw John better placed behind him. A short pass and John dropped a lovely goal. This was positive, attacking, match-winning rugby and from that moment the Lions never looked back. It was their day; their match, and almost their series. In an afternoon they had become the greatest Lions to visit New Zealand!

Gerald Davies scored after nine minutes and John converted and this try was followed by John's own try after 18 minutes, which he converted, and it was 13–0. We rubbed our eyes in the Press Box but it was true... the Lions were winning! The All Blacks steadied and fought back but they had achieved nothing except a few 'near misses' by the interval, although they would play the second half with the wind and the bright sun behind them. At this stage one would have liked another Lions' score for 16 or 18 points.

The second half proved exciting and hard-fought in good spirit but the All Blacks got no more than a try, that was scored by fullback Mains following persistent attacks and rucks in a long siege before the ball went along the line to the right and Mains made the extra man. Apart from this the Lions left no gaps and the forwards did noble work to provide the ball in their own '25' for Edwards or John to clear.

Again, the Lions did not release their firm grip and, as the second half progressed, the more obvious it became that the Lions would win for the All Blacks failed to make use of their possession, as well as failing with two place kicks. It was just not their day. They lost Burgess with concussion after 28 minutes of the second half and Duncan deputised, and although this was unfortunate the match was won and lost by then.

Meads called the Lions the 'greatest touring team he had played against'. Warm praise indeed, while every evening paper was complimentary. It was a pleasure to join Cliff and Gabe David once again at the N.Z.B.C. for the B.B.C. with the victory news. There was champagne for the players, provided by the British Press, and just a glass in the team room and a chat with John Hart, hon. secretary of the F.H.U., supplied the final proof that positive thinking, coaching and team work, had carried the day. The New Zealand side was confused at first and when it did win good ball in the second half had neither the skill nor speed to succeed against a superbly knit defence. No wonder Meads was heard to remark to the referee, 'Give us a break, Ref!' An era had ended for him and New Zealand!

CHAPTER NINE

The Final Test

Team and press flew together from Wellington, of happy memory, to Palmerston North and there they received the biggest reception of the tour, as nearly twenty-five thousand people were 'on parade' to welcome the Lions. The Centennial Committee had done a wonderful job of preparation and after touch-down the party was whisked away to a suburb of the town where the mile-long procession was forming up. There the players were welcomed individually and accompanied to a car or float, to become part of the procession, each sitting with a charming young lady holding a big card with the player's name on it. The British press were accommodated on one vintage fire engine and the New Zealand press on another, so that they were made to feel very much at home and part of the Lions 'circus'. I had never ridden on a fire engine before that day and, although speed was reduced to a 'crawl' long before the show reached the famous square at Palmerston, it was a happy and enjoyable experience.

The square or town centre was the nearest approach to a 'mardi gras' I have seen in New Zealand and, in the centre of it, was a full size replica of the capsule used on one of the astronauts' trips to the Moon. The size of it impressed me but on realising how large is the three stage rocket that sends the capsule into space, perhaps it is a rather confined space to travel so far in!

There was much to do at Palmerston North, for most of us, although the wind from the East blew, and blew with an icy theme. Yet the Sunday evening at the Grand Hotel with Barry John, who drinks very little indeed, as assistant barman, was one of the best of the tour. When several elderly tourists, no longer active as players, retired to bed they were, to say the least, a little unsteady on their legs, but for me it was the happiest celebration in rugby...a Lions second win in a test series in New Zealand!

During the stay at Palmerston, Carwyn, Cliff and myself, did two sessions at the teacher training college; several players visited schools and hospitals and Massey University. Norman Whatman arranged the traditional R.N.V.R. reunion for me and it was pleasant to sit with Alan Stewart, the principal of Massey, Bill Johnstone, Ken Monk and company and talk about the 'dangerous' days, especially at King Alfred and Lancing College! Such friendships are everlasting. Jack Finlay and his charming family entertained Sue, Vivian and myself to dinner and, as always, the 'master gardener', was in good form, as was his good friend Ross Jones. Another special item in Palmerston is the newly opened national rugby museum and John Sinclair, an incredible worker for goodwill between rugby countries, took me to meet the curator and examine some of the wonderful souvenirs presented by the son of the late A. F. Harding, the former Welsh international and captain of the 1908 Anglo-Welsh team. We also met a Mrs Stevens, who is a sister of the late H. B. 'Bert' Winfield of Cardiff, who played full-back for Wales in 1905.

The day of the match dawned cold but dry with clouds threatening and made for the coldest conditions for any of the matches on tour. The Lions were forced to make two changes as Biggar suffered an ear infection and Slattery had not fully recovered from his attack of tonsillitis. Their places were taken by Spencer and Taylor, and this was to be Spencer's tenth and last appearance of the tour.

Twenty-Third Match
Versus Manawatu – Horowhenua at Showgrounds, Palmerston North, August 4.
Lions won by three goals, three penalties and five tries (39) to one penalty and one dropped goal (6).
Weather: Cold and windy. *Ground:* Firm. *Crowd:* 25,000
Teams:
COMBINED XV: J. Francis; J. Karam, J. Brennan, A. McLaren, R. Twentyman; G. Tuarau, B. J. Cuff (capt.); G. Rohloff, G. McKenzie, P. Harris, J. Callesen, M. Oram, J. Betty, R. G. Myers, K. Eveleigh.
BRITISH ISLES: R. B. Hiller; J. C. Bevan, S. J. Dawes, A. J. Lewis, J. S. Spencer; C. M. H. Gibson, R. Hopkins; C. B. Stevens, F. A. L. Laidlaw, J. F. Lynch, W. J. McBride (capt.) W. D. Thomas, J. Taylor, P. J. Dixon, R. J. Arneil.
Referee: Mr R. F. McMullen (Auckland).

ABOVE: The King. A magnificent action picture of Barry John, in the act of following through a kick. Note balance of body and eye following ball after leg has reached top of swing. BELOW: How to play rugby... the wrong way! A striking picture of Muller the Taranaki forward jumping into a ruck which Gibson (hidden) is forming. The flying boot could well have hit Gibson's head. To British eyes, extremely dangerous play, but in some parts of New Zealand they really love it—more's the pity

ABOVE: The Third Test. The first of the two brilliant Lions tries scored against the All Blacks at Wellington and created by Gareth Edwards. Gerald Davies has just grounded the ball over the line after his opposite number Carrington has failed to stop him. BELOW: The second Lions' try in the Third Test, also created by Edwards with a powerful diagonal thrust. He is buried beneath three All Blacks as Barry John dashes over the goal line after receiving from Edwards. In this vital test, John scored 10 of 13 points scored by the Lions

The Fourth Test

This proved to be the coldest match of the tour but also one of the most enjoyable to watch as the Lions laid on a scintillating display. They won comfortably enough by 39 points to 6 and this is always a good sign when it occurs late in any tour, as it suggested the side had retained its fine 'edge' of enthusiasm. As always in New Zealand the local side played hard at first and the forwards played strongly, and caught cleanly at the line-out. Hiller was after the century of points before the end of the tour and Bevan was try-hungry, so the scene was set for entertainment. Again Willie John McBride was honoured as captain which proved extremely popular.

Whether or not the cold conditions reminded the Lions of winter at home, they certainly cut loose after scoring 8 points in 17 minutes and then rushing away before the interval to collect another 14, and so led by 22 to nil when ends were changed. The second half continued in similar manner although the opposition was never as weak as to suggest there was none. It played with spirit and won plenty of ball at the line-out but it was the fine combined skill of the Lions that proved so effective.

When the day ended John Bevan had collected 4 tries to get within one of Tony O'Reilly's 1959 record, and this was most heartening for the young Welshmen who for a number of reasons, but mainly his poisoned foot and injured hands, had gone off the boil a little. His running was strong and resolute again, and he held his passes and his inside backs worked towards him to encourage him. This, at all times, was a feature of the team's approach, for all players endeavoured to help each other and especially those out of form.

The 4 tries gave Bevan 16 for the tour and there remained two provincial matches and the test for him to make his bid for the record, providing he was selected to appear. However, he had only an equal chance with Duckham of winning the left-wing position for the final test, and competition between the two of them was particularly keen although their style and approach was vastly different.

Hiller had a splendid day for he collected 18 points with the wind blustery and awkward. It was such a day as demands accurate skill from a place-kicker, and his orthodox methods revealed how fortunate were the 1971 Lions in having two such players as Hiller and John. Between them they were the scourge of New Zealand provincial sides and, in the tests, John was able to keep the Lions 'in the running' with his kicking and the tourists were not faced with the challenge of Clarke, Williment or McCormick at their best.

As Hiller proved in this match, the 'big boot' was certainly on the British side in 1971 and, following years of watching New Zealand sides kick the Lions off the paddock, it was indeed pleasant for the professional observer. Hiller kicked three conversions, three penalties and scored a try which was an 'All England' performance and brought his tally of points in New Zealand to 91 and to 99 for the tour, which suggested that he would repeat his performance of 1968 in South Africa and cause one to sympathise with him. He was a match-winning player and only the greater full-back skill and strength of John Williams prevented him appearing in a test. Yet Hiller accepted his fate with a smile and never lost his keen sense of humour, while the more one gets to know him, the more interesting a fellow he proves to be.

In scoring eight tries the Lions had indicated, quite clearly, that they intended to win all their provincial matches, even though the remaining two, at Whangarei and Tauranga, promised to be as hard, if not harder, than those that had gone before.

An interesting person at Palmerston North was the referee, R. F. McMullen, who played against the Lions for New Zealand in 1959. A pleasant chap he did quite well, and although he wanted it strictly 'according to the law', there is every promise that he could follow in the footsteps of John Pring and get a test. One sensed throughout the tour that there was a genuine improvement in refereeing and the younger school were more independent and did not allow themselves to be 'talked' into things, (something that Colin Meads did in matches down through the years). This time, John Pring stood no nonsense, and if all New Zealand referees will stop players 'talking' to them, they will grow in stature and be much more appreciated. At the moment they are heading in the right direction.

On Thursday morning we set off for Whangarei in the Northland, where the Lions have always experienced hard times and strong opposition on the field but delightful hospitality off it. Memories came floating in for all those in the party who had made the journey before and especially in 1966 when there was the famous 'Bali hai' party. However, there was one regret about the visit, for one of the best innkeepers in the land had not long died, and the Whangarei Hotel was without Lofty Blomfield, a former wrestler of world class, but his charming widow remained in charge.

It had been raining for ten days in the area and there was threat of 'paddy-field' conditions but, at least the rain ceased when we arrived ahead of the team, who were training in Palmerston North before heading north. Officials at North Auckland are always helpful and Harry Innes, the press liaison officer and chairman Duncan Ross, especially so. However, there was no 'junketing' by players or press, for this was a dedicated tour and everyone was after the prize, no defeats at the hands and feet of the provinces, and the last great challenge was near in the land of the Going brothers, Sid, Ken and Brian. The Lions took no chances and fielded their strongest side, but for Gibson and Duckham.

North Auckland contained five All Blacks, with Sid Going and Richard Guy of the 1971 side, while they were coached by the 'veteran' Ted Griffin who had been coaching the province for over twenty years. I once sat with him, during the 1959, match, when he gave vent to his feelings. In other words, Ted, occasionally, got carried away, but he worked hard with his team and this time he told them to 'give the Lions the hurry up'.

Again, it was another meeting between Sid Going and Gareth Edwards who, with the retirement from big rugby of Ken Catchpole and Dawie de Villiers, were the remaining two of the 'top four'. They had 'battled' away against each other since the Maori match and, as the First Test provided 'no contest' since Gareth was injured, the Second Test saw Going on top, but in the Third Edwards was in charge, and so this match was to be a decider with the Fourth Test to follow. Edwards, fortunately for the Lions, had regained his poise, confidence, full fitness and strength, and, mentally, was attuned to meet the challenge.

Twenty-fourth Match
Versus North Auckland at Okara Park, Whangarei on August 7.
Lions won by one goal and two tries (11) to one goal (5).
Weather: Sunny. *Ground:* Softish. *Crowd:* 30,000.
Teams:

NORTH AUCKLAND: K. T. Going; D. R. Panther, R. R. Jones, J. F. Lynch, J. V. Pullin, J. McLauchlan, W. J. McBride, G. L. Jones, F. J. Colthurst, R. A. Guy, J. S. Kirtlan, C. Poynter, B. Holmes, L. P. Haddon, Z. Marinkovich.
BRITISH ISLES: J. P. R. Williams; D. J. Duckham, S. J. Dawes (capt.), A. J. Lewis, J. C. Bevan; B. John, G. O. Edwards; J. F. Lynch, J. V. Pullin, J. McLauchlan, W. J. McBride, G. L. Brown, D. L. Quinnell, J. Taylor, T. M. Davies.
Referee: Mr P. McDavitt (Wellington).

Fortunately, for everyone, the day dawned beautifully, and one was tempted to take an early morning drive to see friends at Tangowahine, a lovely Maori name meaning 'abducted woman', in the sunshine, but the hotel was 'alive' and everyone was talking about the match and the chances of the Northland. There was no picnic lunch and the press box was packed to capacity, but the band played 'Raindrops'!

The bands at New Zealand rugby grounds are superb for they play well and march with the skill of top rate soldiers while the New Zealand Army Band at the Third Test proved itself the best in the land. Silver and brass bands are popular, and organised and trained with military discipline that is to be admired. They often played 'pop' numbers and I admit to having a liking for 'Raindrops are falling' because the romantic adventures of the trio in the 'Sundance Kid' film, provided excellent escapism from the rigours of a rugby tour!

There were thirty thousand spectators in the new, spacious Okara Park, and a magical air of expectancy, for everyone realised that if the Lions were to have their colours lowered in New Zealand, this was the match, but the Lions were equally determined to survive. This 1971 side had the will, the spirit and the skill, and occasionally, the luck, to survive and the maxim that fortune favours the brave, is certainly true of rugby football.

In this match the Lions got away to a cracking start and were in the lead after three minutes with a splendid try. They moved to the right behind from a line-out and John Williams entered the line to tap the ball on to wing Duckham without actually catching and giving, it was this clever ploy that gave Duckham the chance he needed and away he went like the wind, to beat his opposite number and full-back Ken Going, before scoring a try that was one of his best of the tour. Barry John kicked a lovely goal from near the touch-line and five hyphen nil was the right kind of start in a match that promised to be hard and exciting. Back came the North Aucklanders, breathing fire and brimstone and charging away much more cleverly than other provincial sides. They won the ball and ran at the Lions and exploited well-prepared manoeuvres to suggest that Ted Griffin had decided he would try everything possible to achieve the coveted victory. In defence they tackled and tackled hard and occasionally the Lions dropped passes in midfield.

After 28 minutes of the second half, the North Auckland side equalised with an excellent try and from that moment onwards the match was tense and exciting with the Northland often on the brink of success. They scored when Ken Going entered the line during a passing movement and carved his way through with a strong burst. Jones carried on and slipped the Lions' defence to find Guy up with him and the test prop raced away for 20 yards to score at the posts for Ken Going to kick an easy goal. The score was five-all at the interval, and one felt that if North Auckland took the lead in the second half they would be difficult to overhaul provided they could repeat their efforts of the first half.

As John Dawes said afterwards... 'For the first time on tour I was worried... not how to score ourselves but how to stop North Auckland from scoring!' In the fourth minute of the second half the Lions revealed their true ability for they took the lead they were not to lose. It was John Williams from full-back, who scored the try, from a movement started by Duckham moving infield and then switching. The ball moved out via Dawes and Lewis to John and he had Williams outside him on the right wing. They interpassed cleverly and Williams, cracking on pace, got over the final 20 yards to the corner before the coverers. John could not convert but what a fine try and, more important, a decisive one.

The North were back on the defensive for long periods after this but they did defend magnificently, probably better than any other side against the Lions. Not only did they get one man to the corner flag, but often three, and strong runners like Bevan and Duckham were halted, in desperate but sporting style. It was all hard and exciting but great stuff to watch and the 30,000 crowd gave their side every encouragement, as would the crowd at Llanelli, but they also applauded the Lions. Once the Going brothers executed a dummy and a double scissors, moving blind, and only a superb tackle, his best of the tour, by Williams felled Sid Going to prevent the equaliser. A great moment in the tour!

This was the turning point and in the closing minutes after long pressure the Lions got another try to prove themselves the better of two fine sides. They won a scrum outside the north goal-line and Edwards, who had held his own with his great rival Going, whipped the ball away and perfect passing, gave John Bevan his chance because Williams had entered the line, and the Welsh wing flashed over for his seventeenth try of the tour to equalise the 12-year-old record of the flame-haired Tony O'Reilly, as a Lions try getter in New Zealand.

It had been a great match and proof enough of the resilience of the Lions with their forwards more than holding their own in the second half and showing all New Zealand that the British 'new look' had erased all comments like 'Cream cakes' and 'Lammerton's Lambs'. These 1971 Lions had avenged much of the past but one had to pay tribute to North Auckland for yet again showing their spirit, enthusiasm and 'know-how' as a rugby side. How much better they were in spirit and skill than the Ranfurly Shield holders, Canterbury.

On Sunday the party moved off to Tauranga via Auckland where I stayed for a couple of days to work in the 'silence of my lonely room' and taste the delights of eating at the 'La Boheme'. All work and no play is bad, but it is equally true that on a long tour, neither player nor pressman can afford to 'play up', and that is why it is difficult for some folk to appreciate that tourists are not always available to callers and cannot take a 'drink' or have a 'chinwag' or 'ear-bash' at any time of the day. Sometimes it is a change to talk about other things than rugby football, such as films, books and the theatre!

Tauranga was staging its first big international match as the Bay of Plenty province had to move from Rotorua where the ground was no longer suitable and awaiting rebuilding. Tauranga itself is a lovely holiday resort on the coast and a friendly place. An excellent area in which to launch a long tour.

For this match the Lions did not hold back all their stars in readiness for the test but decided to let them play if they wished to do so. They nominated Barry John, Mike Gibson, Ian McLauchlan and several other candidates and so the side was a more than useful one and, as events were to prove, a necessary one for as in the two previous matches of 1959 and 1966, the Bay were in their most enthusiastic and effective form.

Twenty-Fifth Match
Versus Bay of Plenty at the Domain, Tauranga on August 10.
Lions won by one goal, one dropped goal, three penalties and one try (20) to one goal, one penalty and two tries (14).
Weather: Dry. *Ground:* Firm. *Crowd:* 15,000.
Teams:
BAY OF PLENTY: B. Trask; M. Petterson, E. Stokes, L. Kairpara, G. Moore; G. Rowlands, C. Jacob; J. Helmbright, R. Walker, D. Mohi, G. Hicks, J. Maniapoto, M. Spence, M. Conner, A. McNaughton.
BRITISH ISLES: R. B. Hiller; A. G. Biggar, C. W. W. Rea, C. M. H. Gibson, J. C. Bevan; B. John, R. Hopkins; J. McLauchlan, F. A. L. Laidlaw, C. B. Stevens, W. D. Thomas, G. J. Evans, J. F. Slattery, P. J. Dixon, R. J. Arneil.
Referee: Mr J. P. Murphy (North Auckland).

This was a match which the Lions desperately wanted to win to complete an unbeaten provincial record and become only the second team touring New Zealand to do so. If they were to be known as the 'greatest', and deserve this title which is used all too loosely in sport today, they had to win and prove themselves, as any international side should, better than all the provinces of New Zealand. Without showing any disrespect to the provinces, the overall advantage in skill and combination should be with the touring team providing it is properly coached and led, and has the true spirit of a team. Even on the occasional off-day, the 1971 Lions were always a team – one for all and all for one!

The Lions took the lead with a try by Biggar and followed this with a penalty by Hiller which gave him his 100 points for the whole tour. Then Trask kicked a penalty for the Bay and Hiller got another penalty, before the Bay produced an excellent try by Moore that Trask converted and it was 9–8. This set the fuse to the whole match and it flared liked a jackie-jumper with the crowd yelling and the Lions, at times, hanging on near to the ropes! Still, Hiller was the cool, comfortable player at full-back and another fine penalty, from 45 yards, made it 12-8 at the interval and gave him 100 points in New Zealand. For him it was a splendid show, one deserved by a loyal tourist.

After 10 minutes of the second half the Lions scored from a drop-out, for Arneil fielded the ball when the Bay failed to gather and handed on to McLauchlan, for Hiller to put Gibson away and over for try at the pasts which Hiller converted. Now it was 17-8, but the Bay came back and got an excellent try through Trask but he failed to convert it and a further 40 minutes were played before the Bay, following many exciting attacks, got another try through Walker. Trask's attempt at conversion was just wide and it was 17-14 with injury time to come. There remained, by the clock, seven minutes, and it was in the last of these that Barry John, receiving from a 15 yard scrum, dropped a goal to make victory certain. He therefore beat David Watkins' previous record of seven dropped goals, and maintained his record of having scored in every match in which he appeared.

The Bay had come close to becoming the only province to beat the Lions and it was only superb defence that kept them out on many occasions. They rucked strongly, and handled well behind. They played enterprising rugby while the Lions were often harassed. However, Referee Pat Murphy had a poor day, and was nowhere near test class. The choice for the fourth test had been left open to give him a last minute chance to prove himself, but he was well down the list. A shade passed his best, I would say, and sadly lacking in application of the off-side law.

So there remained one more match, the Fourth and final Test, and a prize beyond compare – a test series and the title of the 'greatest' – enough to call for a super effort on the part of the happy but tired Lions who, for over three months, had worked tremendously hard, with discipline, dedication and excellent spirit, to prove that British Rugby is as good and as enjoyable, and indeed, as effective, as it is anywhere in the world. Yet it was difficult to keep calling for special efforts.

Psychologically, it was hard, very hard, and no one appreciated this more than Coach James but he did it quietly and sensibly, without the 'bull' that accompanies the approach of many successful coaches. He did it cleverly and sincerely, seeking the best ... and he always got the best from his men. This is one of the real reasons for the team's success, for the players were encouraged and helped and guided and always set an example to follow.

The New Zealand selectors had announced their side on the Sunday and it included five changes from the one beaten in the Third Test, with the return of Bryan Williams and Peter Whiting of Auckland. Unfortunately, Alan McNaughton, an excellent flanker from the Bay of Plenty, had been dropped in favour of the harder Tom Lister of South Canterbury, while Phil Gard of North Otago had replaced Joseph in the centre. Mick Duncan of Hawkes Bay who substituted for Burgess in Third Test, held his place and appeared at second five-eighth while Cottrell moved into first and acted as vice-captain to Meads.

The Lions announced their side on Wednesday morning and it was the same as that which had won the Third Test and one could not argue about this choice. The side had proved itself and there was only one doubtful starter in Derek Quinnell whose injured knee was puffed up again and painful. Dixon was asked to stand by and preferred to Arneil when the change was made on the Thursday, and he thus assumed the joint responsibility of keeping Sid Going and Kirkpatrick, reasonably quiet. No easy task, yet a vital one, in the bid to win the series.

Everyone was glad to be back in the Royal International Hotel for several reasons, but it was sad for some that the tour was to end, and one expected a tear or two to fall before the end of the week and the departure for home on Sunday evening! There was shopping to be done, letters to be written, but the McLean family and friends helped with the shopping, while there were farewells to be said and receptions to attend. Vivian and myself headed a party to the Mercury Theatre for an excellent production of the 'Country Wife' and a pleasant party back-stage.

Yet there was plenty of work to do and arrange and the Test provided the last of the 'hot line' reports to Cardiff as the final whistle went for the Special 6 a.m. edition of the *Western Mail*. Rex Reynolds, Alan Wood, Bill Hook and the team in Cardiff worked hard, and this edition was really a special one and I will remember the single word headline for many a year, as it just said ... 'Greatest'!

Enthusiam for the Test was tremendous and tickets could not be obtained, but Link Warren, the most amiable and efficient secretary of the Auckland Union, helped me out, and two friends were extremely grateful as it was a match that everyone wanted to see. The N.Z.R.U., bound by a decision of their clubs, could not show the match 'live' on TV, and so the B.B.C. could not carry out their plan to show it in the early hours of Saturday morning. However, Cliff Morgan did take over the commentary for N.Z.B.C. TV and everyone was reasonably happy in the end, for one felt certain that, in future, the four tests in any series will go out 'live' in New Zealand.

There was a party at Eden Park on Friday evening and a most enjoyable one. Cliff and myself had one last, and pleasant, meal to music at 'La Boheme' with happy company, to forget the pressures of the morrow. For all the Lions party, players and camp followers, it was the BIG one, and the Lions had to win, or at least share a draw as we thought of cheerful, 'Witch Doctor' Smith's forecast... two wins one defeat, and a draw, and the series. He had never wavered... would he be proved right?

Twenty-Sixth Match
Versus New Zealand (Fourth Test) at Eden Park, Auckland, August 14.
Match Drawn: New Zealand one goal, two penalties and one try (14) British Isles one goal, one dropped goal, two penalties (14).
Weather: Cloudy. *Ground:* Firm. *Crowd:* 56,000.
Teams:
NEW ZEALAND: L. W. Mains; K. R. Carrington, M. G. Duncan, P. C. Gard, B. G. Williams; W. D. Cottrell, S. M. Going; B. L. Muller, R. T. Norton, R. A. Guy, P. J. Whiting, C. E. Meads (capt.), T. N. Lister, A. J. Wyllie, I. A. Kirkpatrick.
BRITISH ISLES: J. P. R. Williams; T. G. R. Davies, S. J. Dawes (capt.), C. M. H. Gibson, D. J. Duckham; B. John, G. O. Edwards; J. McLauchlan, J. V. Pullin, J. F. Lynch, G. L. Brown, W. J. McBride, P. J. Dixon, T. M. Davies, J. Taylor.
Referee: Mr J. P. G. Pring (Auckland).

The traditional picnic lunch was much enjoyed by the Welsh press 'mafia' but one was not over-confident of victory for one expected the All Blacks to make a special effort with so much to lose. They had been beaten in South Africa and won only two of their last seven test matches, while they stood to lose their first full test series at home since 1937. The pressure was on them but one assumed it was easier to motivate the All Blacks, for these special reasons and because the country's honour in the rugby game was very much at stake.

The Lions had achieved a half share of the series and an unbeaten provincial record which was far more than anyone had expected from them when they flew out of London in May. They had been highly successful and if the match was lost, as long as it was not lost heavily, then they could return with their heads held high. Yet if they could win or draw, they would become the 'greatest'. In the hour before the kick-off, though an anxious period for both sides, there was greater pressure in the All Blacks' dressing-room, and it provided a last chance for coach-selector Ivan Vodanovich and captain Meads to motivate the All Blacks to raise their game for victory.

Yet as a match it was tense and exciting without the very top skills. For both sides the prize was too great and the occasion too charged with excitement and history to provide the long, flowing, skilful movements. Yet it was tremendously hard and thrilling and even in the press box one could not relax. I recall writing furiously for my 'special story' as well as noting as many details as possible in my match record book. I smoked cigars, big and small, and chewed Mintoes, and nudged Vivian, as the play moved up and down the field. Not many matches have affected me to any degree because the press box is a place for a 'cool head' but there was so much at stake and one did not want to return home yet again, having got so far but not quite to the top.

These 1971 Lions deserved the 'big prize' and there were many in the sporting capacity crowd of 56,000 who also thought so! As expected the match made an explosive start and during the first 15 minutes there were fears that the All Blacks would resort to cave-man tactics and ruin what had proved to be a happy and pleasant series. From the first line-out the ball sailed passed Edwards who turned to follow it but Lister 'chopped' him down. In the next line-out Whiting punched Brown in the eye causing a cut that required five stitches when eventually Brown was forced to retire. It was rough stuff – pointless – unnecessary – and although the All Blacks achieved an eight point lead in the first 13 minutes they did not exactly cover themselves with sporting glory. It was far too tense and vigorous.

Fortunately, one of the best referees produced by New Zealand for many years, following his unhappy baptism in 1966 at Dunedin when Meads 'ran him', John Pring, pulled the match round, getting the players into line, and seeing to it that rugby was the winner and no 'stoush'. Some New Zealanders, but not many, wanted to win by such methods, but another Canterbury in this match would have brought discredit upon New Zealand rugby which would have been a tragedy for all concerned.

Colin Meads put in a word and play resumed a normal, hard, exciting course, to the relief of everyone and the delight of Lions' camp followers. Yet it looked during the first half hour as if New Zealand would win for they were very much on top as their forwards won good ball and the backs moved it cleverly. They were trying desperately hard and the Lions were often pressed in defence. Yet in the last five minutes before the interval the Lions steadied; equalised, and virtually won the series.

After five minutes play in the match the All Blacks scored an excellent try. A pass from Gibson, a rare one to miss, sailed wide of Gerald Davies on the right-wing and Bryan Williams kicked through. The ball was saved outside the Lions line and there followed a scrum. Wyllie stood out to take the pass and handed on to Cottrell who fed Duncan and now the Lions' defence was stretched. Cottrell ran round for the loop and dived over for a try as Gibson tackled him with Carrington spare outside as Duckham had been drawn in to tackle by the overlap. Mains kicked the goal and it was first blood to New Zealand. Eight minutes later, a scrum offence gave Mains a chance of penalty goal from 40 yards and straight over it went for an eight point lead.

John failed with a reasonable penalty attempt inside the New Zealand twenty-five by taking a toe kick, to the surprise of everyone, and was then short with a second attempt from 40 yards on the right touch-line. However, a third attempt after 'hands in the maul' saw him kick a goal and put himself right for the match, as from that moment he did not put a proverbial 'foot wrong'.

Three minutes later, Duckham followed an Edwards kick to the box, where he tackled and robbed Mains in great style to run for the corner and just fail to score, being pushed into touch at the flag but his opportunism had set up a valuable scoring position for the Lions and it was Edwards who was to appreciate this most.

Brown won the ball at the line-out. Down to Edwards it came and he burst away round the open end, handing off forwards. Just short of the line he was tackled but released the ball and Dixon picked up to dive over for the vital try. John kicked the goal and it was eight all as the whistle went for the interval. In five minutes the Lions had recovered from a most difficult position and laid claim to the series. They had revealed, yet again, their major strength... the flair for recovery... the never-say-die spirit!

After two minutes of the second half, the rather stupid act of treading on Dixon in a maul, by the heavyweight and not too clever prop Muller, cost New Zealand three valuable points. John kicked a lovely 40 yard penalty... a beautiful kick... and for the first time the Lions led at 11–8. Seven minutes later, however, New Zealand had equalised. They forced a line-out in the same corner where Duckham ran before the Lions' try. A long throw-in found Lister only half marked and he fell over for a try. Fortunately for the Lions, Mains kicked wide when a conversion then would have proved decisive but it left the score at 11–11.

Nothing could have proved more exciting and one felt that the side to score next would win the match. Within five minutes the Lions were back in the lead. A line-out on the left saw the ball bounce about before Duckham gathered and sent a long pass to midfield where John Williams gathered, turned, and dropped a high goal... how marvellous it looked for the British Isles... and he ran back jumping in the air like George Best and looking to the grandstand where his happy parents were sitting.

There remained 26 or more minutes for play. Could the Lions hold out? Both sides attacked but it was the Lions forwards and Edwards, rather than the backs, who dominated the scene by holding the All Blacks' pack. Edwards and John were in brilliant mood as kickers and all defended well, with John Williams at his best.

The All Blacks tried desperately hard and in the last 20 minutes Delme Thomas substituted for Gordon Brown who left the field after being 'scraped' across knee by 'you know who'. This cut required 14 stitches and the young Scot had proved himself a player of skill and courage. Thomas joined his old team-mate McBride, who was in masterly form as a leader, and the old firm in the second row finished the series in triumph on their last big tour.

Then, after 36 minutes, the Lions fell offside at a scrum, actually it was Dixon, who had played his heart out for his side, who was trapped and Referee Pring had to blow for Mains to kick a 25 yard goal and bring the scores level. Seven more minutes were played and during these hectic and dramatic moments John just failed to win the match when a drop at goal sailed inches wide; Bryan Williams made several brave charges down the wing and Dixon was hurt.

Then the whistle went for time and it was all over. The Lions had won their first series in New Zealand and had become the first Lions side in the twentieth century to win a major series abroad. They were the greatest. They were heroes. They were fine, courageous, skilful, happy rugby players. They had struck a major blow for the cause of British Rugby, for the cause of British sport, and Colin Meads said: 'No other touring team to come to New Zealand will ever do what the 1971 Lions have done!'

It was a magical moment. A triumph for team work and coaching; for the blending of pace and skill in a disciplined approach, without the loss of flair. In the end it was flair and confidence that carried the Lions through and the amazing kicking prowess of Barry John. Yet the Lions could not have succeeded without Willie John McBride and his forwards, who surprised the world with their good sense, skill and courage. Thus it was a team victory and 'Witch' Doctor Smith was right. From the final whistle at Auckland to London Airport, it was Champagne and more Champagne, plus a few tears... but no side deserved the honour more than the 1971 Lions... They were the greatest!

MATCH RECORD

Played 26 Won 23 Drawn 1 Lost 2 For: 580 Against: 231

Day	No.	Date	Opponents	Result	For				Against			
					Goals	Tries	Pens.	Total	Goals	Tries	Pens.	Total
Wed.	1	May 12	Queensland	Lost	1	–	2	11	2†	–	3	15
Sat.	2	May 15	New South Wales	Won	1	2	1	14	–	–	4	12
Sat.	3	May 22	Counties/Thames Valley	Won	3†	1	3	25	–	–	1	3
Wed.	4	May 26	King Country/Wanganui	Won	2	1	3	22	–	2	1	9
Sat.	5	May 29	Waikato	Won	5†	3	1	35	2†	–	2	14
Wed.	6	June 2	N. Z. Maoris	Won	1	–	6	23	–	–	4	12
Sat.	7	June 5	Wellington	Won	7	2	2	47	1†	–	2	9
Wed.	8	June 9	S. Canterbury/N. Otago	Won	2	3	2	25	–	–	2	6
Sat.	9	June 12	Otago	Won	3	–	2†	21	1†	1	1	9
Wed.	10	June 16	West Coast/Buller	Won	6	2	1	39	–	1	1	6
Sat.	11	June 19	Canterbury	Won	1	1	2	14	–	–	1	3
Tues.	12	June 22	M'borough/Nelson	Won	5	2	–	31	–	4	–	12
Sat.	13	June 26	NEW ZEALAND	Won	—	1	2	9	–	–	1	3
Wed.	14	June 30	Southland	Won	5	–	–	25	–	–	1	3
Sat.	15	July 3	Taranaki	Won	3††	–	1	14	–	2	1	9
Tues.	16	July 6	N. Z. Universities	Won	4†	–	3	27	–	2	–	6
Sat.	17	July 10	NEW ZEALAND	Lost	1†	2	1	12	2	3	1	22
Wed.	18	July 14	Wairarapa/Bush	Won	3	4	–	27	–	1	1	6
Sat.	19	July 17	Hawkes Bay	Won	3†	2	2	25	1†	–	1	6
Wed.	20	July 21	Poverty Bay/East Coast	Won	2††	3	1	18	–	1	3	12
Sat.	21	July 24	Auckland	Won	2	-	3	19	1†	–	3	12
Sat.	22	July 31	NEW ZEALAND	Won	3†	–	–	13	–	1	–	3
Wed.	23	Aug. 4	Manawatu/Horo.	Won	3	5	3	39	1†	–	1	6
Sat.	24	Aug. 7	North Auckland	Won	1	2	–	11	1	–	–	5
Tues.	25	Aug. 10	Bay of Plenty	Won	2†	1	3	20	1	2	1	14
Sat.	26	Aug. 14	NEW ZEALAND	Drawn	1	1	2	14	2†	–	2	14

† dropped.

Attendances

1.	Brisbane	11,000
2.	Sydney	22,568
3.	Pukekohe	25,000
4.	Wanganui	23,000
5.	Hamilton	26,000
6.	Auckland	47,000
7.	Wellington	45,000
8.	Timaru	13,000
9.	Dunedin	29,000
10.	Greymouth	4,500
11.	Christchurch	53,000
12.	Blenheim	12,400
13.	Dunedin Test	45,000
14.	Invercargill	22,000
15.	New Plymouth	30,000
16.	Wellington	30,000
17.	Christchurch Test	60,000
18.	Masterton	10,000
19.	Napier	24,500
20.	Gisborne	15,000
21.	Auckland	56,000
22.	Wellington Test	50,000
23.	Palmerston North	25,000
24.	Whangarei	30,000
25.	Tauranga	18,000
26.	Auckland	56,000
	TOTAL	782,968

DETAILS OF SCORERS AND APPEARANCES IN AUSTRALIA AND NEW ZEALAND

Played 26 Won 23 Drawn 1 Lost 2 For 580 Against 231.

	T.	C.	P.	D.	Pts.	App.
John	7	31	28	8	191	17
Hiller	2	25	16	2	110	11
Bevan	18	—	—	—	54	15
Duckham	11	—	—	—	33	17
G. Davies	10	—	—	—	30	10
Biggar	9	—	—	—	27	9
Gibson	5	1	1	1	23	16
Williams	2	2	1	1	16	15
Dawes	5	—	—	1	18	19
Taylor	4	—	—	—	12	15
Spencer	4	—	—	—	12	10
Edwards	3	—	—	—	9	16
M. Davies	3	—	—	—	9	14
Rea	2	—	—	—	6	10
Lewis	2	—	—	—	6	10
Dixon	2	—	—	—	6	15
R. McLoughlin	1	—	—	—	3	5
Quinnell	1	—	—	—	3	10
Carmichael	1	—	—	—	3	6
Hopkins	1	—	—	—	3	11
J. McLauchlan	1	—	—	—	3	18
Evans	1	—	—	—	3	6
	95	59	46	13	580	

Laidlaw (11 matches), Pullin (16), Lynch (15), Brown (14), McBride (15), Roberts (11), Thomas (15), Hipwell (6), Slattery (13), Stevens (6), Arnei (5), did not score.

Test Appearances.

4: J. P. R. Williams, T. G. Davies, S. J. Dawes, C. M. H. Gibson, B. John, G. O. Edwards, J. F. Lynch, J. V. Pullin, J. McLauchlan, W. J. McBride, J. Taylor, T. M. Davies; 3: P. J. Dixon, W. D. Thomas, D. Duckham; 2: G. L. Brown; 1: J. C. Bevan, D. Quinnell, R. Hopkins.

Statistics Of Past Tours

1930:

v. Wanganui	Won	19–3	
v. Taranaki	Won	23–7	
v. Manawhenua	Won	34–8	
v. Wairarapa/Bush	Won	19–6	
v. Wellington	Lost	8–12	
v. Canterbury	Lost	8–14	
v. West Coast/Buller	Won	34–11	
v. Otago	Won	33–9	
FIRST TEST:			
v. Southland	Won	6–3	
v. Ashburton/S. Canterbury/N. Otago	Won	9–3	
	Won	16–9	
SECOND TEST:			
v. N. Z. Maoris	Lost	10–13	
v. Hawke's Bay	Won	19–13	
v. Poverty Bay/Bay of Plenty/East Coast	Won	14–3	
v. Auckland	Won	25–11	
	Lost	6–19	
THIRD TEST:			
v. North Auckland	Lost	10–15	
v. Waikato/Thames Valley/King Country	Won	38–5	
	Won	40–16	
FOURTH TEST:			
v. Nelson/Golden Bay/Motueka/M'borough	Lost	8–22	
	Won	41–3	

21 games played; 15 won, 6 lost, Tests: 1 won, 3 lost.

1950:

v. Nelson/M'borough/Golden Bay/Motueka	Won	24–3	
v. Buller	Won	24–9	
v. West Coast	Won	32–3	
v. Otago	Lost	9–23	
v. Southland	Lost	0–11	
FIRST TEST:			
v. South Canterbury	Drew	9–9	
v. Canterbury	Won	27–8	
v. Ashburton/North Otago	Won	16–5	
	Won	29–6	
SECOND TEST:			
v. Wairarapa/Bush	Lost	0–8	
v. Hawke's Bay	Won	27–13	
v. Poverty Bay/Bay of Plenty/East Coast	Won	20–0	
v. Wellington	Won	27–3	
	Won	12–6	
THIRD TEST:			
v. Wanganui	Lost	3–6	
v. Taranaki	Won	31–3	
v. Manawatu/Horowhenua	Won	25–3	
v. Waikato/Thames Valley/King Country	Won	13–8	
v. North Auckland	Won	30–0	
v. Auckland	Won	8–6	
	Won	32–9	
FOURTH TEST:			
v. N. Z. Maoris	Lost	8–11	
	Won	14–9	

23 games played; 17 won, 5 lost, 1 drawn. Tests: 3 lost, 1 drawn.

1959:

v. Hawke's Bay	Won	52–12
v. East Coast/Poverty Bay	Won	23–14
v. Auckland	Won	15–10
v. N. Z. Universities	Won	25–13
v. Otago	Lost	8–26
v. Sth & Mid Canterbury/North Otago	Won	21–11
v. Southland	Won	11–6
FIRST TEST:		
v. West Coast/Buller	Lost	17–18
v. Canterbury	Won	58–3
v. Nelson/M'borough/Golden Bay/Motueka	Lost	14–20
v. Wellington	Won	64–5
v. Wanganui	Won	21–6
v. Taranaki	Won	9–6
v. Manawatu/Horowhenua	Won	15–3
SECOND TEST:	Won	26–6
v. King Country/Counties	Lost	8–11
v. Waikato	Won	25–5
v. Wairarapa/Bush	Won	14–0
THIRD TEST:	Won	37–11
v. N. Z. Juniors	Lost	8–22
v. N. Z. Maoris	Won	29–9
v. Bay of Plenty/Thames Valley	Won	12–6
v. North Auckland	Won	26–24
FOURTH TEST:	Won	35–13
	Won	9–6

25 games played; 20 won, 5 lost. Tests: 1 won, 3 lost.

1966:

v. Southland	Lost	8–14
v. Sth & Mid Canterbury/North Otago	Won	20–12
v. Otago	Lost	9–17
v. N. Z. Universities	Won	24–11
v. Wellington	Lost	6–20
v. N. Z. Universities	Won	24–11
v. Wellington	Lost	6–20
v. M'borough/Nelson/Golden Bay/Motueka	Won	22–14
v. Taranaki	Won	12–9
v. Bay of Plenty	Drew	6–6
v. North Auckland	Won	6–3
FIRST TEST:		
v. West Coast/Buller	Lost	3–20
v. Canterbury	Won	25–6
v. Manawatu/Horowhenua	Won	8–6
v. Auckland	Won	17–8
v. Wairarapa/Bush	Won	12–6
SECOND TEST:	Won	9–6
v. Wanganui/King Country	Lost	12–16
v. N. Z. Maoris	Lost	6–12
v. Poverty Bay/East Coast	Won	16–14
v. Hawke's Bay	Won	9–6
THIRD TEST:	Drew	11–11
v. N. Z. Juniors	Lost	6–19
v. Waikato	Won	9–3
v. Counties/Thames Valley	Won	20–9
FOURTH TEST:	Won	13–9
	Lost	11–24

25 games played; 15 won, 8 lost, 2 drawn. Tests: 4 lost.